READING QUEST

PRO

A Faithful Guide Through
Your Reading Adventures

DARAKWON

Radu Hadrian Hotinceanu

• MFA degree in Creative Writing from Arizona State University
• BA degree in English & Rhetoric from State University of New York at Binghamton
• Professor of English Language and Literature at Seoul Women's University
• Over 20 years of teaching experience at universities in Korea
• English language editor of *ASIANA Airlines In-flight Magazine*
• Former English language editor of *SPACE* and *Diplomacy* magazines

READING QUEST PRO

Author	Radu Hadrian Hotinceanu
Publisher	Chung Kyudo
Editors	Kim Taeyon, Cho Sangik
Designers	Hwang Sooyoung, Jang Meeyeoun
Photo Credits	pg. 10 (Columbia University Library statue) VIIIPhotography / Shutterstock.com; pg. 24-25 (Sagrada Familia) dimbar76 / Shutterstock.com; pg. 26 (Sagrada Familia) Pit Stock / Shutterstock.com; pg. 27 (Left: interior of Sagrada Famila) Roman Babakin / Shutterstock.com, (Right: interior of Sagrada Famila) Alessandro Colle / Shutterstock.com; pg. 31 (postage stamp) Mitrofanov Alexander / Shutterstock.com; pg. 32-33 (Telecommunications Centre and Post Office) Martyn Jandula / Shutterstock.com; pg. 34 (Geisel Library) Nagel Photography / Shutterstock.com, (Litchfield Towers) Malachi Jacobs / Shutterstock.com; pg. 51 (passenger) Serkant Hekimci / Shutterstock.com; pg. 55 (train) Clay Gilliland / Wikimedia.org; pg. 56-57 (people flying kites) Oleinik Iuliia / Shutterstock.com; pg. 58 (Kites festival) Hanafi Latif / Shutterstock.com; pg. 63 (kids flying kites) wizdata / Shutterstock.com; pg. 64-65 (chess boxing match—boxing round) WCBO / Wikimedia.org; pg. 66 (chess boxing match—chess round) paul prescott / Shutterstock.com; pg. 83 (coin) Gruener Panda / Wikimedia.org; pg. 87 (coins) Gutta100 / Shutterstock.com; pg. 88-89 (*Cloud Gate*) Busara / Shutterstock.com; pg. 90 (*The Sun, the Moon and One Star*) rawf8 / Shutterstock.com; pg. 91 (*The Picasso*) Claudiovidri / Shutterstock.com; pg. 98 (*Fountain*—replica) / Kim Traynor / Wikimedia.org; pg. 104-105 (14th Dalai Lama) Candid168 / Shutterstock.com; pg. 107 (14th Dalai Lama in prayer) Anthony Ricci / Shutterstock.com; pg. 111 (14th Dalai Lama) vipflash / Shutterstock.com

First Published in November 2019
By Darakwon Inc.
Darakwon Bldg., 211, Munbal-ro, Paju-si, Gyeonggi-do 10881
Republic of Korea
Tel: 82-2-736-2031 (Ext. 552)

Price	15,000 won
ISBN	978-89-277-0971-8 14740
	978-89-277-0969-5 14740 (set)

www.darakwon.co.kr

Components	Main Book / Free MP3 Recordings Available Online
	8 7 6 5 4 3 2 22 23 24 25 26

To the Readers

Reading Quest Pro is the second book in a three-book series of readers for adult learners of English. This series contains readings that range from a high-beginning to a high-advanced level. All three books in the series were written with the goal of presenting readings that are interesting, fun, and level appropriate.

Reading Quest Pro is divided into seven units that explore the topics of people in history, architecture, travel, sports, economics, art, and philosophy. Each unit presents two current and engaging stories on a topic. These reading passages are previewed in a Unit Preview section and are further explored in Reading Comprehension, Summarizing Information, Vocabulary in Context, and Reading Connections sections.

The discussion activities in the Unit Preview make this section ideal for classroom use. The Reading Comprehension section emphasizes the development of reading skills such as searching for details and identifying the main topic. The Summarizing Information section gives readers the chance to recall the main points and details of the reading passage through error correction exercises and to practice summarizing the passage in their own words. The Vocabulary in Context section focuses on word analysis skills such as determining the contextual usage of words and understanding the use of phrasal expressions. Lastly, the Reading Connections section provides further information that is relevant to the topic, giving readers the chance to extend their understanding of the reading passages.

Radu Hadrian Hotinceanu

CONTENTS

UNIT ELEMENTS

Each unit of *Reading Quest Pro* includes the following sections and features:

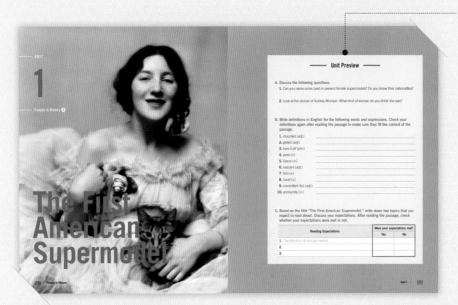

◄ Unit Preview

Three types of activities prepare readers for the reading passage. Readers can check whether their expectations were met after reading the passage by using the anticipation guide table at the bottom of the page.

◄ Etymology

This section explains the origins and meanings of two words or expressions from the reading passage.

Reading Passages ►

Each reading passage has the appropriate sentence length and complexity for the intermediate to low-advanced level.

Quick Questions ►

Quick questions are provided in the margins of each reading passage to encourage readers to consider their comprehension of the passage's details while reading.

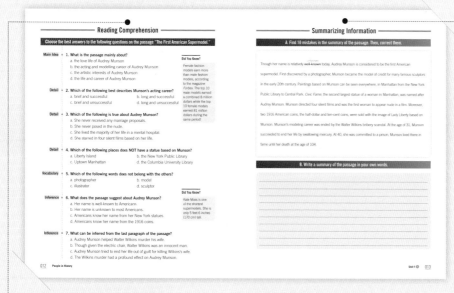

◄ Summarizing Information
Error correction and summary exercises reinforce readers' comprehension of main points and details of the reading passage.

◄ Reading Connections
Every unit includes an additional reading on a topic related to the unit's reading passage. It extends readers' knowledge and provides them with the opportunity for further reflection on the subject.

◄ Reading Comprehension
A set of comprehension questions helps readers test their understanding of the key information of the reading passage.

◄ Vocabulary in Context
Different types of vocabulary exercises provide practice in using the unit's vocabulary in practical contexts.

Did You Know? ►
Fun facts related to the reading passage are presented in a box format on the side of the activities in the Reading Comprehension and Vocabulary in Context sections.

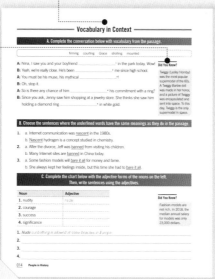

The First American Supermodel

Unit Preview

A. Discuss the following questions.

    1. Can you name some past or present female supermodels? Do you know their nationalities?

    2. Look at the picture of Audrey Munson. What kind of woman do you think she was?

B. Write definitions in English for the following words and expressions. Check your definitions again after reading the passage to make sure they fit the context of the passage.

    1. mounted (*adj.*) _____

    2. gilded (*adj.*) _____

    3. bare it all (*phr.*) _____

    4. pose (*v.*) _____

    5. Grace (*n.*) _____

    6. nascent (*adj.*) _____

    7. firm (*v.*) _____

    8. court (*v.*) _____

    9. committed (to) (*adj.*) _____

   10. anonymity (*n.*) _____

C. Based on the title "The First American Supermodel," write down two topics that you expect to read about. Discuss your expectations. After reading the passage, check whether your expectations were met or not.

Reading Expectations	Were your expectations met?	
	Yes	No
1. *The life of an American model*		
2.		
3.		

01

Q1
What is the name of the largest statue of a woman based on Audrey Munson?

New York City's most famous lady is undoubtedly Lady Liberty, the colossal 46m copper statue on Liberty Island, in New York Harbor. The city's second largest statue of a woman is mounted on top of Manhattan's 40-story Municipal Building and gilded in 24k gold. The golden statue, known as *Civic Fame*, was modeled after a woman named Audrey Munson. While the name Audrey Munson is relatively unknown today, there are few New Yorkers or visitors to Manhattan who have not walked past a statue based on Munson.

Audrey Munson

Munson was born on June 8, 1891, in Rochester, New York. She was blessed with a classical beauty and with the courage to bare it all in the service of art. Munson's beauty was first noticed by photographer Felix Benedict Herzog, who discovered her while she was strolling on Manhattan's Fifth Avenue. After posing for Herzog and other photographers, Munson started modeling for a variety of artists, including sculptor Isidore Konti, painter Francis Coates Jones, and illustrators Harrison Fisher and Charles Dana Gibson, among others. Munson did her first nude modeling job for Isidore Konti.

In 1909, Isidore Konti installed his statue *Three Graces* in the Hotel Astor's Grand Ballroom in Times Square, with all three Graces based on Munson. During the next decade, Munson modeled for a number of statues created by top American sculptors for use in monuments and major public buildings. Statues based on Munson can be found at the New York Public Library on 42nd Street, at the entrance to Central Park (the *U.S.S. Maine* Memorial), in Uptown Manhattan (the Straus Memorial), in front of the Columbia University Library, and in many other places throughout New York City.

Three Graces by Isidore Konti

Columbia University Library statue

Munson's reputation as the model of choice for sculptors and visual artists launched her career in the nascent American film industry. She starred in four silent films: *Inspiration* (1915), *Purity* (1916), *The Girl O' Dreams* (not released), and *Headless Moths* (1921), a film based on her life. Munson was the first woman to appear nude in a movie (*Inspiration*). Her second film, *Purity*, was banned for scenes containing nudity and is the only Munson film that still exists today. The movie studios used lookalike actresses to act Munson's scenes and only used Munson for the nude scenes. Her film career was clearly not a success, so Munson returned to New York in 1916.

The year 1916 was a year of great significance for Munson. That year, the U.S. Mint minted the Walking Liberty Half-Dollar coin with the image of Lady Liberty based on Munson. Munson also appeared on the 1916 ten-cent coin as Winged Liberty, firming her reputation as America's first supermodel. By 1919, Munson was moving in New York's elite society, and wealthy men began courting her.

One such courtship led to her eventual downfall. A certain Walter Wilkins, who fell in love with Munson, murdered his wife in order to marry Munson. Munson denied having a romantic relationship with Wilkins and being involved in the murder. Wilkins was found guilty and given the electric chair. Munson was believed to be innocent, but the scandal ended her modeling career.

By 1922, at the age of 31, Munson was unable to find any more work, so she attempted to end her life by swallowing mercury. At the age of 40, she was committed to a mental hospital, where she lived in anonymity for 64 years until her death in 1996, at the age of 104.

Q2
What launched Munson's career in the movie industry?

Q3
What solidified Munson's reputation as America's first supermodel?

1916 ten-cent coin (top) and half-dollar coin (bottom)

◈ **ETYMOLOGY:** Words Associated with Models ◈

model: The word has its roots in the Latin *modulus*, which means "a small measure or standard." In the 17th century, the word took the meaning of "artist model" or "person whose figure is to be painted or sculpted." The expression "fashion model" has been used since 1904. Currently, a "model" refers to a person who promotes products through video, pictures, or other media.

supermodel: Artist Henry Stacy Marks was the first to use the term "super model" in 1891 in reference to models who delivered energetic, theatrical poses. In 1941, the magazine *Cosmopolitan* used "supermodel" to describe Anita Colby, the highest-paid model at the time. Recent uses of the word refer to a highly paid fashion supermodel who has appeared in the top fashion shows and magazines.

Reading Comprehension

Choose the best answers to the following questions on the passage "The First American Supermodel."

Main Idea

1. **What is the passage mainly about?**
   a. the love life of Audrey Munson
   b. the acting and modelling career of Audrey Munson
   c. the artistic interests of Audrey Munson
   d. the life and career of Audrey Munson

Detail

2. **Which of the following best describes Munson's acting career?**
   a. brief and successful
   b. long and successful
   c. brief and unsuccessful
   d. long and unsuccessful

Detail

3. **Which of the following is true about Audrey Munson?**
   a. She never received any marriage proposals.
   b. She never posed in the nude.
   c. She lived the majority of her life in a mental hospital.
   d. She starred in four silent films based on her life.

Detail

4. **Which of the following places does NOT have a statue based on Munson?**
   a. Liberty Island
   b. the New York Public Library
   c. Uptown Manhattan
   d. the Columbia University Library

Vocabulary

5. **Which of the following words does not belong with the others?**
   a. photographer
   b. model
   c. illustrator
   d. sculptor

Inference

6. **What does the passage suggest about Audrey Munson?**
   a. Her name is well-known to Americans.
   b. Her name is unknown to most Americans.
   c. Americans know her name from her New York statues.
   d. Americans know her name from the 1916 coins.

Inference

7. **What can be inferred from the last paragraph of the passage?**
   a. Audrey Munson helped Walter Wilkins murder his wife.
   b. Though given the electric chair, Walter Wilkins was an innocent man.
   c. Audrey Munson tried to end her life out of guilt for killing Wilkins's wife.
   d. The Wilkins murder had a profound effect on Audrey Munson.

Summarizing Information

unknown
Though her name is relatively ~~well-known~~ today, Audrey Munson is considered to be the first American supermodel. First discovered by a photographer, Munson became the model of credit for many famous sculptors in the early 20th century. Paintings based on Munson can be seen everywhere, in Manhattan from the New York Public Library to Central Park. *Civic Fame*, the second largest statue of a woman in Manhattan, was named after Audrey Munson. Munson directed four silent films and was the first woman to appear nude in a film. Moreover, two 1916 American coins, the half-dollar and ten-cent coins, were sold with the image of Lady Liberty based on Munson. Munson's modeling career was ended by the Walter Wilkins bribery scandal. At the age of 31, Munson succeeded to end her life by swallowing mercury. At 40, she was committed to a prison. Munson lived there in fame until her death at the age of 104.

B. Write a summary of the passage in your own words.

Vocabulary in Context

A. Complete the conversation below with vocabulary from the passage.

firming   courting   Grace   strolling   mounted

A: Nina, I saw you and your boyfriend _____¹ in the park today. Wow!

B: Yeah, we're really close. He's been _____² me since high school.

A: You must be his muse, his mythical _____³!

B: Oh, stop it.

A: So is there any chance of him _____⁴ his commitment with a ring?

B: Since you ask, Jenny saw him shopping at a jewelry store. She thinks she saw him

holding a diamond ring _____⁵ in white gold.

B. Choose the sentences where the underlined words have the same meanings as they do in the passage.

1. a. Internet communication was <u>nascent</u> in the 1980s.

    b. <u>Nascent</u> hydrogen is a concept studied in chemistry.

2. a. After the divorce, Jeff was <u>banned</u> from visiting his children.

    b. Many Internet sites are <u>banned</u> in China today.

3. a. Some fashion models will <u>bare it all</u> for money and fame.

    b. She always kept her feelings inside, but this time she had to <u>bare it all</u>.

C. Complete the chart below with the adjective forms of the nouns on the left. Then, write sentences using the adjectives.

Noun	Adjective
1. nudity	*nude*
2. courage	
3. success	
4. significance	

1. *Nude sunbathing is allowed at some beaches in Europe.*

2. _____

3. _____

4. _____

Reading Connections

Read the following excerpt from a fashion model's diary. Then, do the exercises.

A Day in the Life of a Fashion Model

🎧 02

Today, I had two castings: an open-call casting and a request casting. The agency finally sent me my schedule at 11 o'clock last night. I had planned to meet two of my model friends for coffee, but I had to cancel those plans to get to the castings. I headed to the open-call casting. I got there 10 minutes early, and as soon as I walked in, I put my name on the list. I slipped on my high heels, fixed my hair and make-up, and waited. There were about 50 other models waiting with me. When my name was called, I did my runway walk. The client took a photo of me, which probably meant that he liked me.

That was it. It was all over in about three minutes, so I headed back to the hotel for lunch. I finished my lunch and got to the request casting. A few models were already waiting when I got there. Again, it all went rather quickly. The client asked me to do my walk as he looked over my portfolio. He didn't take my photo but wished me luck anyway. On my way to the hotel, I stopped to meet a friend for coffee. We took photos for our Instagram, and then I walked back to the hotel for dinner and slept. I don't have any castings tomorrow. I hope I get called by the clients at today's castings.

Making Inferences

Check (✓) the statements that can be inferred from the above passage.

1. Request castings usually go faster than open-call castings do. ☐
2. To fashion models, social engagements are more important than work. ☐
3. A fashion model does not walk out of an open-call casting knowing the results. ☐
4. Request castings always guarantee fashion models a job. ☐
5. The large number of fashion models make the modeling profession competitive. ☐

Reflections   Many parents are grooming their children from a very young age—as young as two or three—to become TV and Internet celebrities, such as models, singers, and actors. Is it okay to involve children in the business at such young ages, or are they entitled to enjoy their childhood?

Lord of the China Sea Pirates

Unit Preview

A. Discuss the following questions.

1. What images come to mind when you think of pirates?

2. Ching Shih was one of the most infamous Chinese pirates of all time. She terrorized the China Sea in the early 1800s. What kind of woman do you think she was?

B. Write definitions in English for the following words and expressions. Check your definitions again after reading the passage to make sure they fit the context of the passage.

1. buccaneer (*n.*)

2. intimidate (*v.*)

3. seafarer (*n.*)

4. prostitute (*n.*)

5. brothel (*n.*)

6. squadron (*n.*)

7. behead (*v.*)

8. concubine (*n.*)

9. desert (*v.*)

10. raid (*v.*)

C. Based on the title "Lord of the China Sea Pirates," write down two topics that you expect to read about. Discuss your expectations. After reading the passage, check whether your expectations were met or not.

Reading Expectations	Were your expectations met?	
	Yes	No
1. *A famous and successful female pirate*		
2.		
3.		

Objects associated with sea pirates

The pirates of the Caribbean may be history's most infamous sea thieves, but pirates have been practicing their trade throughout history on all of the world's major bodies of water. From the Cilician pirates that sailed the Mediterranean around the 2nd century B.C. to the medieval Vikings to the Caribbean buccaneers of the 17th century to the current bands of outlaws sailing off the coast of Somalia, pirates have long intimidated merchant seafarers and sailors aboard navy ships.

Q1 What made Ching Shih unique among history's most recognized pirates?

In this world of rugged men with frightening names such as Blackbeard and the Barbarossa brothers, Ching Shih—the pirate lord of the 18th century China Sea—was as tough as they came, though with one major difference: Ching Shih was a woman.

Shih was born in 1775 under the name Shil Gang Xu. She grew up in Guangdong Province in southeastern China, where she became a prostitute on a floating brothel. In 1801, she met Zheng Yi, the pirate lord of the Red Flag Fleet, who took her as his wife and made her an equal partner in running his pirate business.

Q2 How was the pirate fleet of Yi and Shih organized?

Yi and Shih commanded some 200 ships at the time of their marriage, but they soon merged forces with other pirates in the region, which allowed them to grow their fleet to roughly 1,800 ships. The combined fleet was color coded, and it included ships from the leading Red Flag Fleet as well as ships sailing under black, green, blue, yellow, and white flags.

Floating Chinese brothel

The Red Flag Fleet famously defeated a Portuguese squadron of ships in a fight over control of the Portuguese port of Macau.

Yi died in 1807, clearing the way for Shih to take control of the pirate fleet. After Yi's death, Shih adopted her new name, Ching Shih, which literally translates as "Zheng's widow," as "Zheng" is pronounced "Ching." The new pirate lord now had complete control over more than 50,000 pirates.

Shih was a ruthless leader who imposed her authority through a strict code of laws. Anyone violating these laws would be severely punished by whipping and even beheading. Oftentimes, those punished would have their feet nailed to the ship's deck before being beaten. Shih's pirates were allowed to keep wives or concubines aboard the ships, something that was not permitted on the ships of the Caribbean pirates. Loyalty was extremely important to Shih. If any of her pirates deserted, the ship's crew would look for the runaway. If captured, the deserter's ears would be cut off.

Shih's fleet sailed up and down the Chinese coast and collected taxes from coastal villages in addition to raiding any ships encountered along the way, including government ships. The riches captured were evenly divided among the fleet ships.

Ching Shih's rising power was soon noticed by the Qing emperor, who realized he could not defeat her in a war. Instead, the emperor promised to give Shih and her pirates amnesty if they returned to civilized life. As part of the deal, Shih was allowed to keep all of her wealth. Shih accepted the emperor's offer and returned to Guangdong Province, where she remarried and ran a gambling house until her death in 1844.

35

40 **Q3**
How did Ching Shih keep the loyalty of her pirates?

45

50

Ching Shih

◇ **ETYMOLOGY: Words Associated with Pirates** ◇

blackjack: The word originated in the 1500s, when its meaning was "a tar-coated leather jug for beer." In the 1800s, the meaning became "(the black) pirate flag." Since the 1900s, the word has been used for the popular card game. *Example: I like playing blackjack at the casino.*

armed to the teeth: This idiom may have had its origins in the 1600s in Port Jamaica, which was frequented by Caribbean pirates then. Its meaning is "armed with a large number of weapons." Pirates literally held a knife in their teeth for close combat during the boarding of a ship. *Example: The bank robbers were armed to the teeth, so the shootout with the police lasted all morning.*

Reading Comprehension

Choose the best answers to the following questions on the passage "Lord of the China Sea Pirates."

Main Idea • **1. What is the passage mainly about?**

    a. infamous pirates through the ages

    b. the history of pirates in the China Sea

    c. the life of the pirate lord Ching Shih

    d. the life of the pirate lord Zheng Yi

Did You Know?

The eyepatches worn by pirates had nothing to do with missing eyes. They allowed pirates to kept one eye adjusted to darkness, making it easier to fight below the deck of a ship.

Detail • **2. Who were the oldest pirates mentioned in the passage?**

    a. the Caribbean buccaneers   b. the Vikings

    c. the China Sea pirates   d. The Cilician pirates

Detail • **3. Which of the following is NOT true about Ching Shih?**

    a. She took a new name after her husband died.

    b. She died as Zheng Yi's widow.

    c. She was a brutal pirate lord.

    d. She gave up piracy and returned to civilized life.

Detail • **4. What were Ching Shih's pirates NOT allowed to do?**

    a. raid government ships   b. keep concubines on their ships

    c. desert their ships   d. collect taxes from coastal villages

Vocabulary • **5. Which of the following words is different in meaning from the others?**

    a. buccaneer   b. seafarer

    c. pirate   d. outlaw

Inference • **6. What does the passage suggest about Zheng Yi and Ching Shih?**

    a. They shared power but not riches.

    b. They shared riches but not power.

    c. They met while Shih was a prostitute in a floating brothel.

    d. They met during a pirate raid on a ship.

Did You Know?

The word "pirate" comes from the Latin *pirata*, which means "sea robber."

Inference • **7. What can be inferred from the last two paragraphs of the passage?**

    a. The Qing emperor had control over Ching Shih and her pirates.

    b. Ching Shih was afraid to attack the Qing emperor's ships.

    c. Ching Shih's pirates were feared on land as well as on the sea.

    d. Ching Shih lost everything when she returned to civilized life.

Summarizing Information

intimidating

Pirates have been ~~enchanting~~ merchant seafarers and navy sailors from the 2nd century B.C. to the present

time. The lord of the China Sea pirates, Ching Shih, was as rugged as some of history's most generous pirates:

Blackbeard and the Barbarossa brothers. Shih met the pirate lord Zheng Yi while working as a sailor aboard a

floating brothel. Yi and Shih got married and became equal rivals in running the China Sea's most powerful fleet of

pirate ships. Yi and Shih separated their forces with other pirates, creating a combined fleet of some 1,800 ships.

After Yi's arrest, Shih took control of the China Sea's roughly 50,000 pirates. Shih's ruthless authority was based

on a relaxed code of laws that was enforced through severe punishment. Rewards such as whipping and even

beheading kept the pirates loyal and obedient. Shih's pirates helped ships along China's coast and collected taxes

from villages. The Qing emperor made a deal with Shih that allowed her to return to civilized life and to keep her

pirates.

B. Write a summary of the passage in your own words.

Vocabulary in Context

A. Complete the conversation below with vocabulary from the passage.

impose   collect   prostitutes   violated   raided   brothel

A: I heard that the police _____¹ the building across the street.

B: Really? Why?

A: From what I hear, the building was used as a _____².

B: So what happened?

A: They arrested a few of the _____³ who worked there.

B: I guess that's one way for the police to _____⁴ their authority.

A: Do you think they did it because the building owner _____⁵ the law?

B: Yeah. Or maybe because they couldn't _____⁶ any taxes.

B. Choose the sentences where the underlined words have the same meanings as they do in the passage.

1. a. Banks were originally established as safe houses for people's riches.

b. The mountains here are full of riches such as iron ore and coal.

2. a. The farmer was brutally whipped 100 times in public.

b. I don't like a whipped cream topping on my mocha ice coffee.

3. a. Each time she was with him, common sense deserted her.

b. Many soldiers deserted because of fear, hunger, and sickness.

C. Complete the chart below by adding the suffix -ing to each verb to make an adjective. Then, write sentences using the adjectives.

Verb	Adjective
1. accept	*accepting*
2. intimidate	
3. command	
4. impose	

1. *My new college roommates are very **accepting** of my need to practice the violin daily.*

2. _____

3. _____

4. _____

Reading Connections

Read the following passage about a pirate's life. Then, do the exercises.

🎧 04

A Pirate's Life

Pirates rarely reached old age. Life aboard pirate ships was rough, and even the strongest ones fell prey to unforgiving elements: poor hygiene, dehydration—and at times, starvation—and exposure to diseases such as scurvy and dysentery. Scurvy is caused by a deficiency of vitamin C. The diet at sea was very limited and lacked fruits and other sources of vitamin C; therefore, scurvy was a common pirate disease. Its symptoms gave pirates their recognizable look: pale skin, hunched backs, spotted skin, and a lack of hair and teeth. Dysentery was equally common, as it is caused by contaminated food or water. It gave pirates bloody diarrhea, swollen intestines, and other painful symptoms. In addition to diseases, the wounds received from fighting—no matter how small—often proved fatal. As medicine was not available, infections resulted mostly in the amputation of limbs or death. There was also the constant danger of falling overboard during storms or when boarding other ships and drowning. But the biggest danger was perhaps the danger of being captured by authorities. The punishment for piracy was almost always death, and it came in a number of unpleasant choices, such as hanging and beheading.

Making Inferences
Check (✓) the statements that can be inferred from the above passage.

1. Pirates were not as clean or healthy as people who lived on land. ☐

2. Pain caused by disease was a normal part of a pirate's life. ☐

3. Knife wounds were less serious than gunshot wounds for pirates. ☐

4. A pirate would choose capture over scurvy or dysentery. ☐

5. Most pirates experienced peaceful deaths. ☐

Reflections   Today, the word "piracy" is associated with illegalities committed in the Internet world. Many people pirate—take without paying—music, films, or software thanks to various sites that allow downloading without payment, and they argue that people can share freely these services. Should songs, movies and software be shared freely among all people on the Internet?

La Sagrada Familia

Unit Preview

A. Discuss the following questions.

1. Who was Antoni Gaudí? What is La Sagrada Familia, and where is it located?

2. Look at the picture of La Sagrada Familia. Can you guess how long it took to be built?

B. Write definitions in English for the following words and expressions. Check your definitions again after reading the passage to make sure they fit the context of the passage.

1. grandiose (*adj.*) ....

2. entrust (*v.*) ....

3. alter (*v.*) ....

4. make amends (*phr.*) ....

5. curvilinear (*adj.*) ....

6. ongoing (*adj.*) ....

7. facade (*n.*) ....

8. ascent (*n.*) ....

9. imposing (*adj.*) ....

10. ultimate (*adj.*) ....

C. Based on the title "La Sagrada Familia" (The Sacred Family), write down two topics that you expect to read about. Discuss your expectations. After reading the passage, check whether your expectations were met or not.

Reading Expectations	Were your expectations met?	
	Yes	No
1. *The architecture of La Sagrada Familia*		
2.		
3.		

05

Cathedral of La
Sagrada Familia

Q1

What happened
to the original
architectural
design of La
Sagrada Familia?

Q2

Where does the
money for the
construction of La
Sagrada Familia
come from?

If it had a birth certificate, its full name on that document would read "El Templo Expiatorio de la Sagrada Familia," which translates as "The Expiatory Temple of the Sacred Family." To most of us, the architectural masterpiece by Antoni Gaudí is simply known as "La Sagrada Familia" even though it is its full name that does justice to this grandiose Spanish avant-garde church.

Its original architect, Francisco de Paula del Villar y Lozano, had planned to build a Gothic-style church, but when the construction work was entrusted to Antoni Gaudí, the original design went out the window. Gaudí radically altered the building plans, earning himself the title of "the master of modern architecture" thanks to the vision and style of his daring new design.

La Sagrada Familia was initially conceived as a Catholic church but was designated a basilica by Pope Benedict XVI in 2010, a special title given by the Pope to a church for its spiritual, historical, or architectural significance. The expiatory temple part of its name refers to a place of worship that celebrates the amends made by people for their sins.

Construction of La Sagrada Familia began in Barcelona on March 19, 1882. Gaudí's plans envisioned a building that included all the symbols of Christianity and an architectural style that combined elements of Gothic design with curvilinear Art Nouveau shapes. Construction work has been financed by donations made by visitors and the public. Due to the limited funding available, construction is still ongoing, with the final completion date scheduled for 2026, a century after Gaudí's death.

Gaudí was well aware that construction of the basilica would continue long after his death. He once said that this important work was "in the hands of God and the will of the people." The architect focused his construction efforts on the front of the basilica while hoping that future generations would complete the rest of the structure.

Interior views of La Sagrada Familia

Gaudí's construction plan called for three facades: the Nativity Facade, which symbolizes the birth of Jesus Christ; the Passion Facade, which symbolizes the Passion of Christ; and the Facade of Glory, which symbolizes Christ's ascent to Heaven. Each facade would have four bell towers dedicated to the Twelve Apostles of Jesus Christ. Work on the Facade of Glory is ongoing while the other two facades have already been completed.

Aside from the 12 bell towers that rise above the three facades, Gaudí planned six additional towers dedicated to four of the apostles, the Virgin Mary, and Jesus Christ. The Jesus Christ Tower is planned to be the tallest of all these towers with a height of 170 meters.

The interior of La Sagrada Familia is imposing in size and astonishing in style and decoration. The total interior space is approximately the size of a football field at about 120 meters in length and 90 meters in width. The structure is supported by columns in the shape of tree trunks, giving the interior the feel of a forest rather than a church. The interior is arranged in the shape of a cross with five main naves, a basement crypt, an altar, and seven chapels.

Visitors to La Sagrada Familia will notice a lack of straight lines inside the basilica. This type of architecture is known as biomimetic architecture, or architecture that imitates nature. In Gaudí's words, "Originality means returning to origin." And for Gaudí, the origin was nature itself. His ultimate intention for his designs was to replicate nature's perfection.

Q3
What are the main interior spaces of La Sagrada Familia?

◆ **ETYMOLOGY: Words Associated with La Sagrada Familia** ◆

temple: The word comes from the Latin *templum*, which means "an area dedicated to a building used for the worship of a god." The Old English *tempel* means a "building used for the worship of deities (gods)." Currently, "temple" can also describe a Jewish synagogue. *Example: The young Jewish couple had their wedding ceremony performed at the local temple.*

church: The word comes from the Greek *kyrios*, which means "ruler" or "lord." The Greek adjective *kyriakon* means "belonging to the Lord" and was used to describe Christian houses of worship. The Latin *ecclesia* had the same meaning. In Old English, *circe* means "a place of Christian worship" and is similar to the 11th-century French *église*. The word's modern spelling was set in the 16th century. *Example: A Catholic church is much smaller in size than a cathedral.*

Reading Comprehension

Choose the best answers to the following questions on the passage "La Sagrada Familia."

Main Idea 1. **What is the passage mainly about?**

    a. the history and architectural style of La Sagrada Familia

    b. the life and architectural work of Antoni Gaudí

    c. elements of design in Catholic churches

    d. biomimetic architecture in Catholic churches

Detail 2. **Who designed the original plans for La Sagrada Familia?**

    a. Pope Benedict XVI

    b. the master of modern architecture

    c. Antoni Gaudí

    d. Francisco de Paula del Villar y Lozano

Detail 3. **Which of the following styles is NOT found in La Sagrada Familia?**

    a. Gothic   b. Art Nouveau   c. Abstract Art   d. Biomimetic

Detail 4. **Which is the highest structure of La Sagrada Familia?**

    a. the Jesus Christ Tower   b. the Nativity Facade

    c. the Facade of the Glory   d. the Passion Facade

Vocabulary 5. **Which of the following words is different in meaning from the others?**

    a. temple   b. altar   c. church   d. basilica

Inference 6. **What does the passage suggest about Antoni Gaudí?**

    a. He stayed faithful to La Sagrada Familia's original design.

    b. He was convinced that he could finish building La Sagrada Familia.

    c. He believed that architecture should mimic nature.

    d. He designed La Sagrada Familia based on strict geometrical shapes.

Inference 7. **What can be inferred about La Sagrada Familia?**

    a. It has a similar design as other Catholic churches.

    b. Its construction relies on funding from the Spanish government.

    c. It looks exactly the way Francisco de Paula del Villar y Lozano imagined it.

    d. It is considered to be a significant place of worship.

Did You Know?

Work at La Sagrada Familia has continued for the past 137 years... illegally. Antoni Gaudí never received approval to build his church after he applied for a permit in 1882. A building permit was finally granted to the Roman Catholic Church on June 7, 2019.

Did You Know?

Antoni Gaudí was killed by a tram in 1926. He was buried in the underground level of La Sagrada Familia in the chapel of El Carmen Virgin.

Summarizing Information

grandiose

La Sagrada Familia is a ~~mediocre~~ Spanish avant-garde Catholic church. Its architect, Antoni Gaudí, maintained

the plans of La Sagrada Familia's original designer, Francisco de Paula del Villar y Lozano. Pope Benedict XVI

nicknamed La Sagrada Familia a basilica in recognition of its spiritual, historical, and architectural value. La

Sagrada Familia combines elements of Gothic design with linear Art Nouveau shapes. Construction of the basilica

is postponed with its completion date scheduled for 2026. Gaudí's construction plans called for three apostles that

symbolize Christ's birth, passion, and ascent to Heaven. The interior of the basilica is adequate in size, measuring

approximately the size of a football field. The structure is supported by towers in the shape of tree trunks, giving

the church the feel of a forest. This type of architecture is called biomimetic because it rejects nature. Gaudí's aim

was to avoid nature in his designs since he believed that originality meant a return to nature.

B. Write a summary of the passage in your own words.

Vocabulary in Context

A. Complete the conversation below with vocabulary from the passage.

> dedicated   make amends   entrusted   went out the window

A: Jo, how come you didn't show up at the club meeting yesterday?

B: Sorry. My brother stopped by, so all my plans _____ [1].

A: No worries. We _____ [2] a new member with your duties.

B: So did I miss anything exciting?

A: Yeah, we _____ [3] the meeting to you! Just kidding...

B: Well, I'll definitely make the next one.

A: I hope so. And you should _____ [4] by buying all of us pizza.

Did You Know?

Gaudí believed that manmade buildings should not be taller than God's work. That's why the tallest part of La Sagrada Familia—the Jesus Christ Tower—will be one meter lower than Montjuïc, Barcelona's highest mountain.

B. Choose the sentences where the underlined words have the same meanings as they do in the passage.

1. a. Certain microorganisms, such as viruses, <u>replicate</u> themselves.

b. It is illegal to <u>replicate</u> money even if it is done as a form of art.

2. a. Jenny <u>conceived</u> her first child at the young age of 20.

b. The plans for landing on the moon were <u>conceived</u> by NASA.

3. a. Winning Wimbledon is the <u>ultimate</u> accolade for a tennis player.

b. John's <u>ultimate</u> goal in life is to get rid of all of his material possessions.

C. Complete the chart below with the missing adjectives or nouns. Then, write sentences using these words.

Noun	Adjective
1. sin	*sinful*
2.	daring
3. crypt	
4. master	

Did You Know?

La Sagrada Familia is visited by 3 million tourists every year.

1. *Eating this chocolate cake is* **sinful**. *I think my diet has just been ruined.*

2. _____

3. _____

4. _____

Reading Connections

Read the following passage about Antoni Gaudí. Then, do the exercises.

The One and Only
Antoni Gaudí

Antoni Gaudí was as interesting as he was unique. He was a man of contrasts. He was described by some people who knew him as unfriendly and unsocial and by others as friendly, polite, and faithful. The renowned architect spent his whole life as a bachelor. In his younger days, Gaudí dressed smartly and engaged in social events such as visits to the opera. Later in life, he became a vegetarian with a total disregard for his appearance. He wore worn-out clothes and gave all his new shoes to his brother to wear first. He only wore them later as hand-me-downs. The older Gaudí actually looked more like a beggar than a famous architect. Unlike artists such as Pablo Picasso, Gaudí was uninterested in fame and fortune. He was instead deeply devoted to his work and the Christian faith. As a young man, Gaudí suffered from rheumatism and fell ill frequently later in life due to his lengthy religious fasts. Gaudí studied architecture at the Barcelona Higher School of Architecture. His grades were average, however, and he even failed courses on occasion. Actually, while handing Gaudí his diploma during the 1878 graduation ceremony, the school's director famously said, "We have given this academic title either to a fool or a genius. Time will show." Nearly a century and a half later, time has shown that Antoni Gaudí was most definitely an architectural genius.

Making Inferences
Check (✓) the statements that can be inferred from the above passage.

1. Gaudí's genius was unrecognized at the Barcelona Higher School of Architecture. ☐

2. Gaudí did not live the glamorous life of a famous architect. ☐

3. Gaudí's religious faith was more important to him than his personal health. ☐

4. Gaudí was an overachiever as a student. ☐

5. Gaudí stayed single in order to explore a variety of romantic relationships. ☐

Reflections   We commonly think of a personal project as something that can be finished during our lifetimes. Even though La Sagrada Familia was his most important work, Antoni Gaudí never expected to see his church in its final form. What can be said of his personal attitude toward his most beloved project?

Brutalism on the Comeback

Unit Preview

A. Discuss the following questions.

1. What is the most famous building you have visited? Do you know its architectural style?

2. What do you think the purpose of the building depicted in the picture is?

B. Write definitions in English for the following words and expressions. Check your definitions again after reading the passage to make sure they fit the context of the passage.

1. whimsical (*adj.*) ....

2. bow out (*phr.*) ....

3. reinforce (*v.*) ....

4. modular (*adj.*) ....

5. ravages (*n.*) ....

6. prefabrication (*n.*) ....

7. austere (*adj.*) ....

8. decay (*v.*) ....

9. eyesore (*n.*) ....

10. vandalism (*n.*) ....

C. Based on the title "Brutalism on the Comeback," write down two topics that you expect to read about. Discuss your expectations. After reading the passage, check whether your expectations were met or not.

Reading Expectations	Were your expectations met?	
	Yes	No
1. *The origins of Brutalism*		
2.		
3.		

Q1

Why do trends come and go with the times?

Trends are representations of the whimsical nature of human desires. But trends are often short lived, being victims of their own success. People will adopt a trend in the hope of being unique only to abandon it when they realize that everyone else is doing it. Trends come and go the same way in fashion, music, and even architecture. Brutalism is an architectural style that became trendy in the 1950s before bowing out like a bad musical act in the late 1970s.

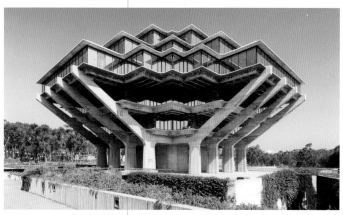

Brutalism is a harsh term for something involving style. At the very least, you would not expect something aesthetically pleasing. The Brutalist style involved the heavy use of reinforced concrete and steel elements. The word brutalist comes from the French *béton brut*, which means "raw concrete." Buildings designed in this style were grandiose and geometric and were mostly used as government buildings, schools, libraries, theaters, and housing projects.

Geisel Library, University of California, San Diego

To trace the origins of Brutalism, we have to go back to a building built in Marseilles, France, in 1952 and named Unité d'Habitation. Its designer was the Swiss-French architect Le Corbusier, who was very fond of using concrete. Unité d'Habitation was a gigantic housing complex that provided living space for 1,600 people. Le Corbusier's design involved modular apartments fit inside a reinforced concrete framework. The building looks like it was put together from oversized concrete Lego blocks.

Q2

How can Brutalism be described in terms of style?

The building's lack of ornaments and its rigid geometry laid the foundations for the Brutalist style. This style fit the time period. During the 1950s, countries in Europe and around the world were rebuilding after the ravages of World War II, and Brutalism provided a perfect way to rebuild. Reinforced concrete was relatively cheap and durable, and prefabrication sped up the construction process. The Soviet Union and the Eastern European communist countries in particular used this architectural style as a way to advance their socialist ideal of providing equal housing for the masses. Brutalism became the architecture of socialism.

Litchfield Towers, Pittsburgh, Pennsylvania

Western countries also employed Brutalism, especially in urban housing projects for the poor. But these buildings looked and felt austere and unwelcoming. Their heavy coats of concrete did not age well. Concrete is known to crumble, decay, and retain water stains, making it look awful if not properly maintained. A single such building can become the eyesore of an entire neighborhood. It is not difficult to see why Brutalism fell out of favor with architects and builders. In the Western world, Brutalism came to symbolize the urban decay of poor neighborhoods. Brutalist buildings were often covered in graffiti, either as acts of vandalism or expressions of art. This led to the further deterioration of these buildings. By the late 1970s, Brutalism was out.

Q3
Why haven't Brutalist buildings aged well?

But Brutalism refused to die. As a matter of fact, in the past few years, people seem to have regained interest in this form of architecture. Conservation societies are doing their utmost to prevent Brutalist buildings from being demolished. Meanwhile, the hashtag #brutalism has over 500,000 images. What is the reason for this late resurgence? Brad Dunning of *GQ Magazine* has an intriguing take on it: "Brutalism is the techno music of architecture, stark and menacing. Brutalist buildings are expensive to maintain and difficult to destroy. They can't be easily remodeled or changed, so they tend to stay the way the architect intended. Maybe the movement has come roaring back into style because permanence is particularly attractive in our chaotic and crumbling world."

Velasca Tower, Milan, Italy

ETYMOLOGY: Words Associated with Brutalist Architecture

eyesore: Both "eye" and "sore" have their origins in Old English—the Saxon *eage* and the Old Norse *sarr*, respectively. The compound noun "eye-sore" was used by Shakespeare in *The Taming of the Shrew* in its modern context. *Example: The torn grass on the football field is an eyesore to the whole campus.*

vandalism: The name for this act of destruction originates from the Vandals, a Germanic tribe that sacked Rome in 455. Since the 17th century, a "vandal" has meant someone who "willfully destroys anything that is beautiful or venerable." *Example: Vandalism of subway train cars with graffiti paint was popular in New York in the 1980s.*

Reading Comprehension

Choose the best answers to the following questions on the passage "Brutalism on the Comeback."

Main Idea • 1. What is the passage mainly about?
a. the beginning and end of Brutalism
b. the Brutalism aesthetic and its most famous buildings
c. the major criticisms of Brutalist buildings
d. Brutalism and its contemporary resurgence

Did You Know?

Prince Charles is not a fan of Brutalism. He once called Britain's Brutalist buildings "more offensive than rubble." On the other hand, Zaha Hadid, the designer of the Dongdaemun Design Plaza (DDP), is an admirer of Brutalist architecture.

Detail • 2. Which of the following adjective pairs is NOT connected to Brutalism?
a. attractive and ornate
b. stark and menacing
c. grandiose and geometric
d. austere and unwelcoming

Detail • 3. What is the main cause for the deterioration of Brutalist buildings?
a. their minimalist design
b. the tendency of concrete to decay and to retain water stains
c. the use of prefabrication in the construction process
d. their use as schools, libraries, theaters, and government buildings

Detail • 4. Why do trends go out of style, according to the passage?
a. They are victims of Brutalism.
b. Their popular qualities are lost.
c. Their unique qualities are lost.
d. They are replaced by human creativity.

Vocabulary • 5. Which of the following words is different in meaning from the others?
a. permanence
b. resurgence
c. comeback
d. revival

Inference • 6. What does the passage suggest about Brutalism?
a. Western countries used it to advance their socialist ideals.
b. Eastern countries used it to provide urban housing for the poor.
c. It provided a convenient way to rebuild after the ravages of World War II.
d. It died out due to the urban decay of poor neighborhoods.

Did You Know?

Some of the villains in early James Bond movies, such as the villain in *Goldfinger*, were based in gigantic Brutalist buildings.

Inference • 7. What can be inferred about Brutalism from the passage?
a. Its permanence is desired in our chaotic world.
b. Its association with techno music makes it popular.
c. Brutalist buildings are expressions of art.
d. Brutalism is the architecture of urban decay.

Summarizing Information

Trends in architecture, art, and fashion appear and ~~emerge~~ *bow out* in the same way. The Brutalist style of architecture involves the heavy use of reinforced steel. Buildings designed in this style are grandiose and curvilinear. Le Corbusier, a Brutalist architect, was reluctant of using concrete in his works. His Unité d'Habitation design made use of shabby apartments that looked like oversized Lego blocks. Prefabrication of these concrete blocks was cheap and slowed down the construction process. For these reasons, Brutalism satisfied the socialist ideal of providing equal housing for the privileged. Western countries also built Brutalist buildings, mostly in rural housing projects. Most Brutalist buildings have become eye-catchers in their neighborhoods due to the decay and water stains in their concrete coating as well as graffiti vandalism. Brutalism has made a comeback, however, as Brutalist buildings are difficult to destroy, and this permanence makes them undesirable in our chaotic and crumbling world.

B. Write a summary of the passage in your own words.

Vocabulary in Context

A. Complete the conversation below with vocabulary from the passage.

vandalism   housing project   out of favor   austere   decay

A: When I was young, we lived in a tall, ugly building in a _____¹.

B: Do you remember much from those days?

A: Yes, the apartment, playground, and everything else felt so _____².

B: That style of housing fell _____³ many years ago, right?

A: That's true because buildings _____⁴ if you don't take care of them.

B: Was it safe to live there?

A: Most of the time. But graffiti _____⁵ and robberies were common.

B. Choose the sentences where the underlined words have the same meanings as they do in the passage.

1. a. My boyfriend is so whimsical; I never know what he'll do next.

b. I love Jenny's whimsical sense of humor.

2. a. The laws of physics are not as rigid as we think.

b. During the movie, Kiki's face was rigid with horror.

3. a. The framework of this old car is still solid and rust free.

b. The framework for his ideas was described in his biography.

C. Complete the chart below with the missing adjectives or nouns by adding or removing -ing. Then, write sentences using these words.

Noun	Adjective
1. ravages	*ravaging*
2. decay	
3.	menacing
4.	interesting

1. *The **ravaging** effects of the tornado could be seen all over the town. No house was left standing.*

2. _____

3. _____

4. _____

Read the following passage about Brutalist websites. Then, do the exercises.

🎧 08

Brutalist Websites

The term "Brutalism" was applied to a style of architecture that sacrificed comfort and aesthetics for the sake of functionality. Brutalism was concerned more with materials such as concrete and steel and less with appearance. These characteristics of Brutalist architecture are also applied to website design. Websites that are minimalist and focus on functionality rather than frivolity fall into the Brutalist category. The younger generations may find such websites unattractive and displeasing to the eye, but Brutalist websites can be very successful from a commercial point of view as they appeal to an audience that focuses on the content they provide rather than the way the content is provided. Take, for instance, the popular website Craigslist. It is as Brutalist as they come. There are no pictures, no videos, and no cute graphics or animations on Craigslist. The website displays only stripped-down information in a throwback to the 1990s era of the Internet. The main construction materials there are hyperlinks, boxes, and text. These materials are as unappealing as concrete and steel yet are just as effective. Do you want your information displayed fast? Do you want to get straight to the point without using time-consuming Flash apps? This website does just that. And yes, it is commercially successful.

Making Inferences
Check (✓) the statements that can be inferred from the above passage.

1. Aesthetics are central to Brutalist architecture and website design. ☐
2. Members of the younger generation tend to focus more on the way content is provided. ☐
3. Craigslist is commercially successful because it appeals to members of the younger generation. ☐
4. Craigslist uses hyperlinks, boxes, and text to deliver content quickly to users. ☐
5. Hyperlinks, boxes, and text are as appealing as concrete and steel. ☐

Reflections   Online and traditional media are overrun with images that compete for aesthetic perfection. It seems that many people all over the world are preoccupied with looking good. Do you care more about functionality or design when you buy a product?

3

The Pearl of
the Adriatic

Unit Preview

A. Discuss the following questions.

1. The picture shows an old town on the Adriatic Sea. Do you know the location of the Adriatic Sea?

2. Do you know the name of the city shown in the picture? What about the country?

B. Write definitions in English for the following words and expressions. Check your definitions again after reading the passage to make sure they fit the context of the passage.

1. walled (*adj.*) ....

2. rugged (*adj.*) ....

3. fortification (*n.*) ....

4. juxtaposed (*adj.*) ....

5. vantage point (*n.*) ....

6. uber- (*prefix*) ....

7. spare (*v.*) ....

8. breach (*v.*) ....

9. (shining) beacon (*n.*) ....

10. quarantine (*n.*) ....

C. Based on the title "The Pearl of the Adriatic," write down two topics that you expect to read about. Discuss your expectations. After reading the passage, check whether your expectations were met or not.

Reading Expectations	Were your expectations met?	
	Yes	No
1. *The name and location of a beautiful city on the Adriatic*		
2.		
3.		

Lord Byron once called it "the Pearl of the Adriatic," and George Bernard Shaw described it as a "paradise on Earth." Both were referring to Dubrovnik, a medieval walled city designated by UNESCO as a World Heritage Site.

Q1

What was Dubrovnik's status during the Middle Ages?

Dubrovnik is situated on the Adriatic Sea under the rugged Srđ Mountain, at the southernmost tip of Croatia. During the Middle Ages, Dubrovnik was part of Ragusa, a merchant state that rivaled Venice for economic prosperity in the Mediterranean region. In 1918, Ragusa's name was changed to Dubrovnik after the city-state became part of the Kingdom of Yugoslavia.

Dubrovnik's Old Town, also known as Stari Grad, is surrounded by a stone wall constructed in the 14th century. The wall stretches for a mile and a half and is supplemented by two round towers, 14 square towers, and a few fortifications. Dubrovnik's houses, churches, palaces, monuments, and museums are all crafted from the same light-colored limestone as the wall surrounding them, which creates a magical contrast with the vibrantly red-colored tiles that cover these structures. When that color is juxtaposed with the purple-blue tones of the Adriatic Sea, you can easily imagine how breathtaking the sunsets can be from any vantage point in Dubrovnik.

Q2

By what name is Dubrovnik also known thanks to a popular TV show?

People around the world, and especially in the United States, may know Dubrovnik by another name: King's Landing, the capital of Westeros in HBO's hit show *Game of Thrones*. Being chosen as the shooting location for this uber-popular TV series has certainly increased Dubrovnik's fame around the world, and, consequently, the number of visitors it draws yearly. Dubrovnik was also a shooting location for the movie *Robin Hood: Origins*.

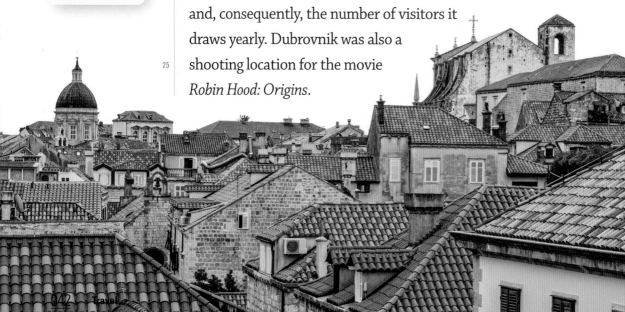

The walled Old Town, Dubrovnik

Dubrovnik itself has seen enough real history unfold inside and outside its walls long before TV and Hollywood added their narratives. The English king Richard the Lionheart contributed a large sum of money toward the building of Dubrovnik's Cathedral of the Assumption after surviving a frightful storm off the Croatian coast at Dubrovnik during his return from the Third Crusade in 1192. The English king apparently had promised God that he would build the cathedral if his life were spared during the storm.

Dubrovnik's Cathedral of the Assumption is one of the city's many historical attractions, but none is more recognizable and symbolic than the city's stone walls. The walls that surround the Old Town have never been breached in any attack on the city by a foreign army and for good reason: The walls are as thick as six meters in some places.

Dubrovnik has always been a pioneering city. Its innovative spirit was a shining beacon for Europe and humanity during the times when the world was plunged into the intellectual and cultural darkness of the medieval era: Dubrovnik's Franciscan monastery, founded in 1317, houses one of the first and oldest pharmacies in the world; Dubrovnik's sewage system, installed in 1296, is still in use to this day; Dubrovnik established one of the world's first quarantine facilities in 1377 and one of the first orphanages in the world in the Monastery of St. Clare in 1432.

Dubrovnik is a small city with a population of around 42,000, but the Pearl of the Adriatic is a heavyweight when it comes to tourism, attracting over a million tourists a year. With so many visitors eager to discover Dubrovnik's marvels, there is a fear held not only by locals but also by others that the city may be losing its soul.

35

Q3
What fact stands as evidence to the sturdiness and strength of Dubrovnik's walls?

40

Dubrovnik's Cathedral of Assumption

45

50

◆ **ETYMOLOGY: Words Used in Descriptions of Dubrovnik's Architecture** ◆

monument: The word comes from the Latin *monumentum,* which means a "memorial structure," "statue," "tomb," "record," or literally "something that reminds." The word was first used in its present spelling in Old French in the 13th century and in its present meaning in English in the 17th century. *Example: The Pantheon in Rome is a monument dedicated to the past Roman gods.*

tower: The word comes from the Latin *turris,* which means "a high structure" or "tower." The word was first used in Old English as *torr*, in French as *tour*, and in Spanish and Italian as *torre*. The present English spelling may be a combination of these spellings. *Example: The Eiffel Tower is an imposing iron structure that measures 324 meters in height.*

Reading Comprehension

Choose the best answers to the following questions on the passage "The Pearl of the Adriatic."

Main Idea

1. What is the passage mainly about?

    a. The beauty and location of Dubrovnik

    b. Dubrovnik's historical buildings

    c. Dubrovnik's history and tourist attractions

    d. Dubrovnik's innovative and pioneering spirit

Detail

2. What was Dubrovnik formerly known as?

    a. Paradise on Earth

    b. Ragusa

    c. the Kingdom of Yugoslavia

    d. Stari Grad

Did You Know?

Dubrovnik is separated from Croatia by a 12-mile strip of land belonging to Bosnia and Herzegovina. Visitors driving to Dubrovnik from the north must pass through border control in Bosnia and Herzegovina's port city of Neum.

Detail

3. Why did Richard the Lionheart help build Dubrovnik's Cathedral of the Assumption?

    a. God ordered him to do so.

    b. He had made a promise to God.

    c. It was a gift for returning victorious from the Third Crusade.

    d. He wanted to build a shelter from a frightful storm.

Detail

4. Which of the following is true about Dubrovnik's walls?

    a. They can be as thick as 6 meters.

    b. They were frequently breached in wars.

    c. They were constructed in the 17th century.

    d. They are made of purple-blue limestone.

Vocabulary

5. Which of the following words is different in meaning from the others?

    a. museum   b. fortification   c. wall   d. tower

Inference

6. What does the passage suggest about Dubrovnik?

    a. Its thick walls have recently been restored.

    b. It has never enjoyed economic prosperity.

    c. It is in danger of losing its identity due to an influx of tourists.

    d. It owes its history to the popular TV show *Game of Thrones*.

Did You Know?

Dubrovnik was the first European state to recognize the United States of America in 1783.

Inference

7. What can be inferred about the Old Town?

    a. Its location makes it inaccessible to international tourism.

    b. Its historical value has never been recognized internationally.

    c. It was destroyed repeatedly by invading armies.

    d. It makes a great filming location for movies set in medieval times.

Summarizing Information

designated
Dubrovnik was ~~constructed~~ as a World Heritage Site by UNESCO. The city is located on the Adriatic Sea coast

under the smooth Srđ Mountain. Before 1919, Dubrovnik was known as Ragusa, which was a military state

during the Middle Ages. Dubrovnik's Old Town is an area surrounded by a fence made of light-colored limestone

as thick as six meters in some places. Dubrovnik's houses, churches, palaces, monuments, and museums are all

painted from the same light-colored limestone as the wall surrounding them. Dubrovnik's buildings are covered

by roofs whose vibrant red color creates a magical mix with the purple-blue tones of the Adriatic Sea. In the 12th

century, the English king Richard the Lionheart helped build Dubrovnik's Cathedral of the Assumption, one of its

main entertainment attractions. Recently, Dubrovnik was used as a travel location for the popular TV series *Game

of Thrones* and the movie *Robin Hood: Origins*. Dubrovnik's innovative spirit has shown the world one of the first

examples of a pharmacy, a medieval water supply system, and a quarantine facility. As this medieval towered city

gets more than a million tourists every year, there is concern that Dubrovnik may be losing its soul.

B. Write a summary of the passage in your own words.

Vocabulary in Context

A. Complete the conversation below with vocabulary from the passage.

be spared   vibrantly   shining beacon   quarantine   narrative

A: I was reading your _____¹, and I have questions about the story.

B: Sure. What are you unclear about?

A: It's about this part where Antonio asks for his life to _____².

B: What about it?

A: Antonio is sort of a _____³ for those around him, right?

B: True. He inspires everyone with his _____⁴ worded speeches.

A: So they save him by putting him in _____⁵ in an isolated hospital?

B. Choose the sentences where the underlined words have the same meanings as they do in the passage.

1.   a. As soon as we opened up the curtains, we saw the <u>breathtaking</u> scenery outside.

   b. Tom's <u>breathtaking</u> arrogance shocked everyone at the meeting.

2.   a. Mike Tyson was a <u>heavyweight</u> boxing champion during the 1980s and 1990s.

   b. Despite his early death, John Lennon was a <u>heavyweight</u> of the music industry.

3.   a. After four days of fighting, Napoleon <u>breached</u> the opposing Russian army.

   b. The CEO <u>breached</u> a previous agreement between the companies.

C. Complete the chart below by writing synonyms to the adjectives on the left. Then, write sentences using the adjectives.

Adjective	Synonym
1. magical	*fascinating*
2. frightful	
3. recognizable	
4. innovative	

1. *Her shelves were stocked with* **fascinating** *books about science.*

2. _____

3. _____

4. _____

Reading Connections

The letter below was sent to and published in the U.K. periodical *The Independent* on August 31, 1992. The events in the letter took place between 1991 and 1992 during the Croatian War of Independence. Read the letter. Then, do the exercises.

🎧 10

Sir,

For almost a year now, the population of Dubrovnik has been subjected to incredible suffering and human degradation. A large area of the municipality is still under the occupying force of the Serbian-Montenegrin army. Refugees within the city number 17,000 while in the occupied territory, there are about 3,500 prisoners in Cavtat and Konavle. News from these areas can be obtained only with great difficulty. But this news is about the physical and psychological abuse of which the wider world is still ignorant. Homes have been transformed into concentration camps. We, they, are at the end of the extreme tether of endurance. Reservists from Montenegro are in power there today, and their methods are astonishingly brutal. Before now, houses were robbed and destroyed; but as we write, homes are being demolished within the presence of their owners, owners who are taken away by night for questioning. Then they are usually kept as prisoners. There are confirmed reports of murder. Robbery is endemic in the streets; only wedding rings are not stolen. All boats and cars have been stolen. In the hotels, only the bedsteads remain. The area has no water; but this means nothing to the occupying army. They stubbornly refuse to pass our deliveries of water on to the citizens of Cavtat and Konavle. Croatian money is banned. People have to exist only on the humanitarian aid which arrives every week from the city of Dubrovnik. Public movement is limited, too. People cannot gather together, and a curfew starts at 8 p.m. Candles must not be seen. Windows must be closed. You are forbidden even to go on to your own gardens or terraces. All letters, messages, and parcels are opened and censored. Many never arrive. Stealing is routine. Every attempt to open an office for UN and EC monitors has failed. This is happening in the heart of your Europe and ours in the age of the New World Order. Please, after so many months, help us to restore our respectability and our human rights to live and work under conditions acceptable to the world at the end of the 20th century.

Yours sincerely,

AIDA DIRLIC and B. SIMATOVIC

Making Inferences

Check (✓) the statements that can be inferred from the above passage.

1. The Serbian-Montenegrin army occupied and controlled parts of Dubrovnik. ☐

2. In the occupied areas, people felt free and secure in their homes. ☐

3. The Montenegrin reservists were brutal during their occupation of Dubrovnik. ☐

4. The letters, messages, and parcels of the occupying army were censored. ☐

5. The writers of this letter are appealing to help from a free and democratic Europe. ☐

Reflections Democratic countries often neighbor countries where brutal regimes are in power. This is true for Europe, South America, Africa, the Middle East, and Asia. Think of North and South Korea and of China and Taiwan for examples in Asia. Should democracies ignore the human rights abuses that go on not far from them?

Epic Train Journey on the Trans-Siberian Railway

Unit Preview

A. Discuss the following questions.

1. What do you know about Siberia's location and climate?

2. What is the longest train ride you've taken? How long do you think the Trans-Siberian journey is?

B. Write definitions in English for the following words and expressions. Check your definitions again after reading the passage to make sure they fit the context of the passage.

1. understated (*adj.*)

2. extremity (*n.*)

3. epic (*adj.*)

4. commence (*v.*)

5. unforgiving (*adj.*)

6. terrain (*n.*)

7. address (*v.*)

8. notable (*adj.*)

9. ornate (*adj.*)

10. taiga (*n.*)

C. Based on the title "Epic Train Journey on the Trans-Siberian Railway," write down two topics that you expect to read about. Discuss your expectations. After reading the passage, check whether your expectations were met or not.

Reading Expectations	Were your expectations met?	
	Yes	No
1. *Facts about Russia's Siberian region*		
2.		
3.		

11

Q1
Why is the Trans-Siberian Railway important to Russia?

Russia is a country that spans two continents and eleven time zones. Nothing in this country is understated. It is only fitting that it boasts the world's longest railway: the Trans-Siberian Railway. This is the artery that has been pumping Russia's cultural, industrial, military, and spiritual blood from its heart in Moscow through its huge body, stretched across ancient forests, flower-filled meadows, gentle hills, jagged mountains, mighty rivers, and bottomless lakes, to its Oriental extremity in Vladivostok ever since its creation. The 9,289km route from Moscow to Vladivostok is both epic and unforgettable.

Construction on a railway linking the Russian capital Moscow with the resource-rich Siberia and the Pacific port city of Vladivostok commenced in the 1880s at the direction of Tsar Alexander III. Due to a limited budget and challenging engineering requirements presented by the unforgiving terrain and harsh weather conditions of the Russian Far East, the initial line was built to very low standards. It was not until the late 1920s that all of its shortcomings were adequately addressed, making the railway fully functional.

Q2
Who benefitted from the Trans-Siberian Railway during World War II?

The Trans-Siberian Railway's function proved vital during World War II as it supported in turn both sides of the forces in conflict. Prior to the Nazi invasion of Russia, the railway had served as an economic and military link between Japan and Germany; after the attack on Russia, the railway served as a similar link between the U.S. and its European allies. The railway's economic importance continued after the war and remains important even today as one-third of Russia's exports are shipped on the line. Presently, despite the increased convenience of air travel, thousands of Russians still depend on the line for transportation between cities scattered across the vast Russian landscape.

The Trans-Siberian journey can start even earlier than Moscow in the city of St. Petersburg. The notable cities along the way include Nizhny Novgorod, a World Cup 2018 city; Yekaterinburg, a historic

A Trans-Siberian train

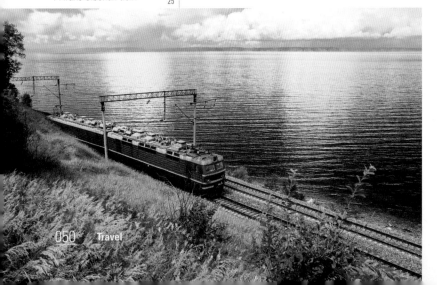

city where the last Russian Tsar and his family were murdered by the Bolsheviks in 1918; and Krasnoyarsk, described by Russian novelist Anton Chekhov as "the most beautiful Siberian city." Aside from these, numerous smaller towns give the traveler a taste of the real Russia and its language. Zima, meaning "winter" in Russian, is one such example. Another town has the more challenging name of Uyarspasopreobrazhenskoye.

A passenger looking outside from the train

The Trans-Siberian Railway crosses 16 important rivers. Of these, the longest—and the seventh longest in the world—is the Ob River while the widest, at 1.9km across, is the Amur River. It also passes through a 2km tunnel, the Tarmanchukan, and along the shores of the deepest and one of the largest lakes in the world, Lake Baikal, which holds some 20% of the world's fresh water.

Among the must-see attractions along the Trans-Siberian Railway are Slyudyanka Station, which is the only train station in the world built entirely of marble; Ulan-Ude, the capital of the Siberian Buryat Republic, which is a territory belonging to the Buryat indigenous people, and the nearby Ivolginsky Datsan, a Tibetan Buddhist monastery; historical Irkutsk with its fascinating churches, museums, and ornate log cabins; and perhaps most importantly, the immense Russian panoramas of unending taiga, forests of larch, silver fir, pine, and birch trees topped by an endless sky that provides spectacular sunrises and sunsets. For this last reason alone, there is hardly a bucket list around without a journey on the Trans-Siberian Railway.

Q3
What is the most important attraction seen from the Trans-Siberian line?

◆ ETYMOLOGY: Words Related to Train Journeys ◆

railway: The word originates from the Latin *regula*, meaning "rule" or "a straight piece of wood." The 14th century French word *reille*, meaning "bolt" or "bar," added to the meaning. The English "way" was added to these in 1776 to make "railway," which meant a "road that uses wooden rails for easy transportation." The modern meaning of "train tracks" was established around 1812. *Example: A railway track will soon connect our city to the capital.*

train: The word originates from the Latin *traginare*, a derived form of *tragere*, which means "to pull." In Old French, "trainer" means "to pull or drag" usually a gown or a cloak. In the 15th century, "train" came to mean "succession or progression." The meaning of "locomotive attached to cars" was first recorded around 1816. *Example: Steam trains powered the Industrial Revolution.*

Reading Comprehension

Choose the best answers to the following questions on the passage "Epic Train Journey on the Trans-Siberian Railway."

Main Idea • 1. What is the passage mainly about?

 a. the origins of the railway linking Moscow with Vladivostok

 b. the history and attractions of Siberia

 c. the history and attractions of the Trans-Siberian Railway

 d. the touristic value of the Trans-Siberian Railway

Did You Know?

Due to its sensitive military installations, Vladivostok was off-limits to all foreigners until 1990, and even Russian (Soviet) citizens had to get a special permit to visit it.

Detail • 2. Which of the following word pairs does NOT appear in the passage?

 a. spiritual blood   b. historic city

 c. deepest river   d. endless sky

Detail • 3. Which of the following is NOT true about the Trans-Siberian Railway?

 a. It connects St. Petersburg with the Far East city of Vladivostok.

 b. Its length exceeds 9,289km.

 c. Its shortcomings were resolved at the end of the 1920s.

 d. Its construction was initiated by the Bolsheviks.

Detail • 4. Which of the following is NOT a city on the Trans-Siberian line?

 a. Tarmanchukan   b. Ulan-Ude

 c. Zima   d. Uyarspasopreobrazhenskoye

Vocabulary • 5. Which of the following adjectives is different in meaning from the others?

 a. notable   b. immense   c. huge   d. vast

Inference • 6. What does the passage suggest about the Russian Far East?

 a. It lacks natural resources.

 b. It has a gentle climate.

 c. It is home to Russians and people of other ethnicities.

 d. It is located close to Moscow and St. Petersburg.

Did You Know?

The Tibetan Buddhist monastery Ivolginsky Datsan has been visited by the Dalai Lama on a number of occasions.

Inference • 7. What can be inferred about Russia from the passage?

 a. It is an undeveloped and backward country.

 b. It is not well suited for tourism.

 c. Its territory contains many of the world's geographical features.

 d. Not many travelers want to visit it.

Summarizing Information

A. Find 10 mistakes in the summary of the passage. Then, correct them.

Russia is a huge country that stretches across two ~~countries~~ *continents* and 11 time zones. The Trans-Siberian Railway connects the Russian capital Moscow with Vladivostok, a city in its Oriental vicinity. The Trans-Siberian Railway was initially built to high quality due to a limited budget, an unforgiving terrain, and moderate weather conditions. During World War II, the Trans-Siberian Railway fought in turn both sides of the forces engaged in the war. Presently, the line remains important for the shipping of exports and for the transporting of people between Russia's clustered cities. The Trans-Siberian Railway stops in modern cities such as Yekaterinburg as well as smaller towns such as Zima. The Trans-Siberian Railway goes under Russia's longest and widest rivers and passes along the shores of the world's deepest lake. An immense panorama of unending jungle topped by an endless sky can be seen from the train. The quick journey on the Trans-Siberian Railway is easily found on most people's bucket lists.

B. Write a summary of the passage in your own words.

Vocabulary in Context

bucket list   panoramas   shortcomings   taiga   harsh

A: Jen, what are you up to?

B: I'm writing my _____ ¹. You know, things I need to do.

A: So what have you written down so far?

B: For one, some of the _____ ² I need to correct about myself.

A: That's useful. What else?

B: A journey through the Siberian _____ ³ by train.

A: You'll have to deal with some _____ ⁴ weather there, you know.

B: Yeah, but just think of the beautiful _____ ⁵ for my Instagram!

Did You Know?

Because he was afraid of flying, David Bowie used the Trans-Siberian Railway to return to the U.K. after his 1973 tour of Japan. He had first crossed the Sea of Japan by ferry.

B. Choose the sentences where the underlined words have the same meanings as they do in the passage.

1. a. The president is scheduled to <u>address</u> the nation on TV tonight.

    b. I tasked the IT team to <u>address</u> the flaws in our latest software.

2. a. The doctor said he suffered frostbite in every <u>extremity</u> of his body.

    b. Tierra del Fuego is a desolate land at the <u>extremity</u> of Argentina.

3. a. Engineers have made some <u>notable</u> improvements to the bridge.

    b. A <u>notable</u> art piece at the show is a sculpture by Giacometti.

C. Complete the chart below by writing antonyms to the adjectives on the left. Then, write sentences using the adjectives.

Adjective	Antonym
1. understated	*flashy*
2. unforgiving	
3. epic	
4. ornate	

Did You Know?

Each train carriage on the Trans-Siberian usually has a *provodnitsa* (female attendant) who cleans, maintains the hot water dispenser, and puts out steps at stations.

1. *Movie stars always seem to live in **flashy** homes in exotic locations.*

2. _____

3. _____

4. _____

Reading Connections

Read the following passage about the Rossia Nr. 2 train. Then, do the exercises.

Rossia Nr. 2

 12

The Rossia Nr. 2 train is the name of a Trans-Siberian train that connects Moscow with Vladivostok. It is classified as a fast train and makes a minimum number of stops in smaller towns. On the Trans-Siberian Railway, you will use either a Russian, Mongolian, or Chinese train, depending on your final destination. These trains usually provide first-, second-, and third-class service.

The first class (*Spalny Vagon*) cars have two beds in each compartment and nine lockable compartments per car. The beds are arranged in a bunk-bed format with a small sofa on Chinese or Mongolian trains or as two lower beds on Russian trains. There are two washrooms and toilets per car. The second class (*Kupe*) has four beds per cabin and nine compartments per car. There are two washrooms and toilets per car, and the compartments are lockable. The third class (*platskartny*) has an open-plan bed arrangement with 54 bunks per car arranged in bays of four on one side of the aisle and bays of two on the opposite side. There are no lockable compartments in this class.

Some trains provide a service car, which has a pay-for shower and Internet as well as a laundry service, but this type of car is not always available. Showers are available in every compartment only in the first-class sections of trains #3 and #4. Each car, whether first, second, or third class, has a bathroom with a toilet and a small sink and is serviced by a couple of attendants called *provodnik* (male) or *provodnitsa* (female) who check tickets, provide bedding, and tend to the free hot water dispenser called *samovar*. All cars have at least one or two power sockets next to the toilets, and first-class and newer second-class cars offer individual sockets in each compartment. An attached restaurant car serves drinks, snacks, and affordable full meals—less than $20 for two courses and a couple of bottles of beer.

The Trans-Siberian trains are generally safe although one should not openly display valuables. Each car has one or two conductors who check tickets and are responsible for safety. In addition, most trains have a police team on board.

Making Inferences
Check (✓) the statements that can be inferred from the above passage.

1. All Trans-Siberian trains are similar in appearance and functions. ☐

2. Modern conveniences such as Internet service are provided on all Trans-Siberian trains. ☐

3. The first-class cars are the least crowded and are followed by the second-class ones. ☐

4. First- and second-class cars provide better safety than third-class cars. ☐

5. *Provodnitsa* and *provodnik* are similar to flight attendants on airplanes. ☐

Reflections   There is an old Russian expression that says, "The slower you go, the farther you will be." This seems to be the case, in a figurative way, for the Trans-Siberian Railway. Its relative slow speed of about 80km/hr allows travelers to experience Russian culture and to make human connections. But will the Trans-Siberian Railway be inevitably replaced by a bullet train?

Competition
Kite Flying

Unit Preview

A. Discuss the following questions.

1. The picture shows a kite festival held in a park. Does your country have any kite festivals?

2. In this country's state of Gujarat, kite flying is the most popular sport. Which country is it?

B. Write definitions in English for the following words and expressions. Check your definitions again after reading the passage to make sure they fit the context of the passage.

1. talisman (*n.*) ....

2. ward off (*phr.*) ....

3. maiden (*n.*) ....

4. twine (*n.*) ....

5. be laced with (*phr.*) ....

6. stunt (*n.*) ....

7. feature-packed (*adj.*) ....

8. choreography (*n.*) ....

9. intricate (*adj.*) ....

10. compulsory (*adj.*) ....

C. Based on the title "Competition Kite Flying," write down two topics that you expect to read about. Discuss your expectations. After reading the passage, check whether your expectations were met or not.

Reading Expectations	Were your expectations met?	
	Yes	No
1. *The history and origin of kites*		
2.		
3.		

13

A group of Balinese at the Bali Kite Festival

Some sports will make you shout, "Wow!" and the exclamation would be a sign of surprise or wonder. But there is a sport that will have you say, "Wow," in quite a literal sense: kite flying. That's because *wao* means "kite" in the Thai language.

Kite flying has been practiced in Asia since antiquity. It is believed that kites were flown in China as long as 3,000 years ago. During the 7th century, Japanese Buddhist monks brought kites to Japan and used them as talismans to ward off evil spirits. Thai farmers have flown kites for over 700 years believing that their high-flying kites could help them get good harvests. In India, meanwhile, miniature paintings from the 15th and 16th centuries show young men flying kites that drop love messages into the waiting hands of their chosen maidens.

Throughout history, kites have been flown for religious practices, secret communications, celebrations, and even competitions. Recently, the flying of kites as part of organized sports competitions has become an increasingly popular attraction around the world.

One of the earliest known examples of competitive kite flying comes from the *Malay Annals*, a fictional history of the Malay Empire. It is said that Rajah Ahmad, the eldest son of a 15th-century Malaccan sultan, cut all the flying kites out of the sky with a powerful kite flown from a strong fishing twine one day. Rajah kept cutting kites day after day until his kite met the smaller kite of a man named Hang Isa Pantas. Hang's kite, however, had a big secret: Its twine was laced with powdered glass. This allowed it to cut the more powerful twine of Rajah's kite.

Kites were brought to Europe during the 16th century by Dutch merchants who had traveled to the Malay peninsula. At first, kites in Europe were mostly used by children who were playing. In 1972, however, Englishman Peter Powell perfected a dual-line stunt kite and used it as a form of sport involving acrobatic movements of kites.

Q1
According to historical fiction, who was one of the first men to fly kites competitively? Who defeated him in this sport?

Q2
What is Peter Powell known for in the sport of kite flying?

Today's kites are feature-packed with multi-lines, agile shapes, and advanced materials. Competitions involve complex choreographies, much like intricate ballet dances in the sky. Competitors are judged on their performances in compulsory set routines as well as their artistic interpretation of music, which is quite similar to figure skating. These performances are made by individuals or teams of up to eight pilots, who synchronize the flights of their kites within centimeters of one another.

Kite-flying competitions are held at the national and international level, and there is even an annual world championship of kite flying called the World Sport Kite Championship (WSKC). It is the most prestigious competition in the sport-kiting world. Participants come from countries around the world and compete for three days in the "precision" and "ballet" disciplines, with an international judging panel scoring each performance.

Q3
How often is the World Sport Kite Championship held?

Kite-flying competitions are also held at kite festivals that are staged in cities across the world. The Weifang International Kite Festival is held in China in April each year, and it includes a world kite championship, a 10,000-person kite performance, and the Weifang Kite-Flying Championship. Meanwhile, the Bali Kite Festival is held in Indonesia in July or August. The competition involves traditional kites, modern kites, and even innovative three-dimensional kite designs. The Wildwoods International Kite Festival takes place in the U.S. in May and includes the East Coast Stunt Kite Championship and an indoor kite competition. The U.S. actually has a National Kite Flying Day, on February 8, and a National Kite Month, in April, when every day is an opportunity to fly a kite for fun or in competition.

A Malaysian traditional moon kite

◆ **ETYMOLOGY: Words Associated with Kite Flying** ◆

duel: The word comes from the Latin *duellum*, meaning "war." In Medieval Latin, *duellum* specifically refers to combat between two people. In the late 15th century, the French *duelle*, or the Italian form *duello*, had the meaning of a "single, judicial combat," as in two people fighting in front of two witnesses to settle a score or to get justice. Since the 16th century, the English "duel" has had the general sense of a "contest between two parties." The modern usage retains that meaning. *Example: The two rappers challenged each other to a "battle rap," a sort of vocal duel set to musical beats.*

stunt: The present meaning of the word comes from the 19th century American usage of "an act made to attract attention." This is perhaps derived from the colloquial "stump," meaning "to dare or challenge." The expression "movie stuntman" was first used in 1930. *Example: Evel Knievel is the most famous daredevil of all times. His motorcycle stunts are legendary.*

Reading Comprehension

Choose the best answers to the following questions on the passage "Competition Kite Flying."

Main Idea

1. What is the passage mainly about?
   a. the history and practice of flying kites in competitions
   b. kite flying festivals and competitions around the world
   c. the invention and development of kites
   d. the rules and format of competitive kite flying

Detail

2. How did Hang Isa Pantas defeat Rajah Ahmad's more powerful kite?
   a. by cutting kites from the sky day after day
   b. by lacing the twine of his kite with powdered glass
   c. by flying his kite from a strong fishing twine
   d. by being the eldest son of a 15th-century Malaccan sultan

Detail

3. Which of the following is true about kite flying competitions?
   a. They involve intricate ballet dances in the sky.
   b. Competitors are judged solely on artistic interpretation of music.
   c. They are held at the national and international level.
   d. They don't allow kites made from advanced materials.

Vocabulary

4. Which of the following words is different in meaning from the others?
   a. performance   b. championship   c. tournament   d. competition

Detail

5. What did Japanese Buddhist monks use kites for?
   a. warding off maidens   b. getting good harvests
   c. dropping off messages   d. chasing away evil spirits

Inference

6. What does the passage suggest about kite-flying competitions?
   a. They are based on the concept of two kites dueling each other.
   b. They are mostly popular in Asia, where the sport originated.
   c. They have certain requirements similar to those in figure skating.
   d. They are only held between individual competitors from different countries.

Inference

7. What can be inferred from the passage about kite-flying festivals?
   a. All of them are held during April, the International Kite Month.
   b. They are focused mostly on indoor performances and competitions.
   c. They offer a chance to showcase traditional as well as modern kite designs.
   d. Competitions at the festivals are restricted to modern kites.

Did You Know?

The Chinese general Han Hsin of the Han Dynasty (206 B.C.-220 A.D.) flew a kite above a city to calculate the distance he would have to tunnel past the city's fortified walls. Having determined the exact distance, his troops were able to dig the tunnel and conquer the city.

Did You Know?

In 1822, English inventor George Pocock built a carriage pulled by a pair of large kites steered by four lines. His carriage reached speeds of up to 20 miles per hour.

Summarizing Information

religious

Kites have been flown since antiquity for ~~medical~~ practices, communications, celebrations, and even

competitions. Chinese, Japanese, Thais, and Indians have flown kites for reasons such as warding off bad

spirits, communicating in secret, and helping farmers get better recipes. The *Malay Annals* describe a kite dance

between Rajah Ahmad and Hang Isa Pantas won by the latter due to a clever improvement to his kite. After kites

were brought to Europe, Englishman Peter Powell created a dual-line kite that could perform tumbles as a form

of sport. Modern kites are feature-packed with multi-lines, lazy shapes, and advanced materials. Competitors

are required to complete complex choreographies during free set routines that involve artistic interpretations of

music. These are either individual or team performances where team members watch the flights of their kites.

Participants at the famous World Sport Kite Championship compete for three days in the precision and ballet arts.

Kite-flying festivals are currently criticized in cities around the world. Due to the sport's increasing obscurity, the U.S.

even has a National Kite Flying Day, on February 8, and a National Kite Month, in April.

B. Write a summary of the passage in your own words.

Vocabulary in Context

A. Complete the conversation below with vocabulary from the passage.

intricate   panel   feature-packed   compulsory   choreography

A: Are you watching the Olympics? Figure skating is on.

B: I'm watching Alina Zagitova's _____¹ performance. Wow!

A: Yeah, the _____² is great—all those cool dance moves!

B: And the design of her dress is so _____³. Amazing colors, too.

A: What score did she get in the _____⁴ part?

B: I'm not sure, but the _____⁵ of judges seemed very impressed.

A: I think she'll win the gold for sure.

B. Choose the sentences where the underlined words have the same meanings as they do in the passage.

1. a. Hollywood actor Steve McQueen performed his own driving stunts in the movie *Bullitt*.

   b. The group's latest video is so bad that we can only hope it is a publicity stunt.

2. a. Some people hang a rabbit's foot in their cars as talisman in the hope of avoiding accidents.

   b. Tottenham FC has found a talisman in Son Heungmin, a true goal-scoring machine.

3. a. The *Titanic's* maiden voyage ended in disaster when it struck an iceberg.

   b. Jenny's maiden name changed to Smith after she got married.

C. Complete the chart below by writing phrasal verbs with "off" that match the definitions on the left. Then, write sentences using the phrasal verbs.

Definition	Phrasal Verb
1. to scare away	*ward off*
2. to pay a debt in full; to result in profit	
3. to display proudly	
4. to delay; to postpone	

1. *Native Americans use dreamcatchers to **ward off** evil spirits while they sleep.*

2. _____

3. _____

4. _____

Read the following passage about Korean kites. Then, do the exercises.

Fighting Kites in the Korean Sky

🎧 14

Traditional Korean kites are called *yeon* and are distinguished by their design, shape, and color. All in all, over 100 types of *yeon* have been launched in the Korean skies since around the early 7th century. Traditional kites such as *bangpae* kites are commonly used in kite-fighting competitions by Korean kite enthusiasts.

The *bangpae* kite was traditionally made with handmade mulberry paper and bamboo sticks, but its contemporary versions can be made of lightweight fabric such as nylon and sticks made of composite materials. The *bangpae* kite has a rectangular shape with a circular hole in the center of the fabric that controls air flow, five sticks that give structure to the kite, and sometimes a tail. The kite is tethered with a single string controlled by a reel.

Bangpae kites are often dueled against one another with opponents trying to cut the opposite kite's tether line by using their own kite's tether line. The kites are flown at least 50 feet in the air. The kites can be decorated in many colors and themes, ranging from traditional designs using Chinese and Korean calligraphy to more modern themes and designs.

Making Inferences
Check (✓) the statements that can be inferred from the above passage.

1. Korea has a long history of flying kites. ☐

2. Koreans have been dueling kites for many hundreds of years. ☐

3. *Bangpae* kites have a rectangular hole in the middle. ☐

4. Modern Korean kites are built the same way as their ancient predecessors. ☐

5. Korean kites are limited in types, designs, and colors. ☐

Reflections   Kites remind us that we have always dreamed of flying. These seemingly simple wind toys have inspired us to build complicated machines such as airplanes, rockets, and space shuttles. Today, perhaps we need kites for simpler purposes or perhaps for more important ones. Can you think of any?

The Eclectic Sport of Chess Boxing

Unit Preview

A. Discuss the following questions.

1. Do you know any international boxing champions? How about famous chess champions?

2. Can you think of some sports that are a combination of two sports?

B. Write definitions in English for the following words and expressions. Check your definitions again after reading the passage to make sure they fit the context of the passage.

1. bareknuckle (*adj.*) _____

2. chariotry (*n.*) _____

3. eclectic (*adj.*) _____

4. fortitude (*n.*) _____

5. proposition (*n.*) _____

6. depiction (*n.*) _____

7. stalemate (*n.*) _____

8. level (*adj.*) _____

9. inception (*n.*) _____

10. storied (*adj.*) _____

C. Based on the title "The Eclectic Sport of Chess Boxing," write down two topics that you expect to read about. Discuss your expectations. After reading the passage, check whether your expectations were met or not.

Reading Expectations	Were your expectations met?	
	Yes	No
1. *The history and development of chess boxing*		
2.		
3.		

Q1

How was Roman boxing different from Greek boxing?

Boxing was a sport as far back as the 7th century B.C., when the ancient Greeks made it part of their Olympic games. The Romans later improved the sport by introducing leather gloves, which made it safer compared to the bareknuckle boxing practiced by the Greeks. The earliest known evidence of
5 Roman boxing comes from a pair of leather boxing gloves dating back to 120 A.D., which were discovered in England near Hadrian's Wall.

Chess is an intellectual sport whose origins can also be traced back to antiquity. The earliest evidence of chess points to 6th-century-A.D. India. This early form of Indian chess was called *chaturanga*, literally meaning "four
10 military divisions": infantry, cavalry, elephantry, and chariotry. The divisions correspond to the present-day pawn, knight, bishop, and rook, respectively.

Q2

In what way is chess boxing similar to the biathlon?

The two sports could not be more different from each other. One involves intellectual agility while the other demands physical power and nimbleness. Put them together, however, and you have a rather eclectic hybrid sport called
15 chess boxing. The chess boxing fighters must show fortitude of body and mind, which makes this sport quite a tough proposition. Chess boxing is not the first nor the only hybrid sport in existence. The biathlon is an example of a much older and well-established hybrid sport.

The idea of chess boxing is credited to Iepe Rubingh, a Dutch performance
20 artist. Rubingh, inspired by a depiction of a chess boxing championship in a comic book by Enki Bilal titled *Froid Équateur,* staged an artistic performance of chess boxing with his friend Jean Louis Veenstra in a Berlin art gallery in 2001. The two later met in a real match as Iepe the Joker versus Louis the Lawyer in the final match of the sport's first professional tournament in Amsterdam, in 2003. Also in 2003,

A 2011 chess boxing match in Berlin, Germany

Rubingh formed and became the president of the sport's first professional organization, the World Chess Boxing Organization (WCBO).

A chess boxing match involves 11 alternating rounds of boxing and speed chess. The winner of the chess phase is decided through a checkmate, a fighter exceeding the individual time limit of 12 minutes allowed for the chess phase, or a fighter failing to make a move within 10 seconds of a time warning issued by a referee. Alternatively, the winner of the boxing phase is decided by a knockout or referee decision. If the chess phase ends in a stalemate, the fighter with the highest score on technical points awarded from the boxing phase is the winner. If the fighters are level on technical points, the one using the black pieces in the chess phase is declared the winner. A fighter can win both phases if his opponent retires.

Since its inception, chess boxing has grown its following outside its country of origin, Germany, to countries across Europe and Asia, particularly Russia and India. This should come as no surprise as the two countries are renowned for producing top chess players and, in the case of Russia, top boxers.

The world has heard plenty from boxing legends Manny Pacquiao and Conor McGregor or from storied chess champions Garry Kasparov and Bobby Fischer. Is the world prepared to hear from boxing chess champions such as WCBO European champion Tihomir "Tigertad" Titschko and GBCBO champion Tim Woolgar? Is their sport entertaining enough to establish a worldwide fandom? These answers will surely be revealed in time. For now, chess boxers will have to keep punching above their weight.

Q3

How is a chess boxing winner decided in the case of a stalemate and the same number of technical points for both fighters?

Chess boxing, a hybrid sport that is a combination of chess and boxing

◆ **ETYMOLOGY**: Words Associated with Chess ◆

checkmate: This check expression used for an attack on the opposing king with no escape comes from the Arabic *shah mat*, meaning "the king has died." The Old French *eschec mat* and the more modern French form *échec et mat* as well as the Spanish *jaque y mate* and the Italian *scacco-matto* all contain the meaning of "the king has died." *Example: "After an hour of nail-biting play, Jensen moved his rook in front of the black king and declared checkmate."*

pawn: The meaning of the word comes from the medieval Latin *pedonem*, meaning "foot soldier," itself derived from the Latin *pedonem*, which means "a person going on foot." The meaning related to chess comes from the late 14th-century Anglo-French *poun*. *Example: Each chess player has a small army of 10 pawns ready to sacrifice themselves for the king and the queen.*

Reading Comprehension

Choose the best answers to the following questions on the passage "The Eclectic Sport of Chess Boxing."

Main Idea 1. **What is the passage mainly about?**

a. the competitive nature of chess boxing

b. the origins and present state of chess boxing

c. the rules and format of chess boxing

d. past and present chess boxing champions

Did You Know?

Chess boxers wear headphones during the chess phase of the match in order to silence the noise of the crowd and commentators.

Detail 2. **Who fought against the Joker in the first chess boxing tournament?**

a. Enki Bilal

b. Iepe Rubingh

c. Jean Louis Veenstra

d. Conor McGregor

Detail 3. **How can a chess boxing fighter lose a match?**

a. by exceeding the individual time limit allowed for the chess phase

b. by knocking out his opponent in the boxing phase of the match

c. by forcing a checkmate on his opponent in the chess phase of the match

d. by scoring more technical points in the case of a chess stalemate

Detail 4. **Which of the following individuals is most likely NOT a chess player?**

a. Manny Pacquiao

b. Tim Woolgar

c. Tihomir Titschko

d. Garry Kasparov

Vocabulary 5. **Which of the following words is different in meaning from the others?**

a. foot soldiers
b. pawns
c. knights
d. infantry

Inference 6. **What does the passage suggest about chess boxing?**

a. It has been around since the times of the Greeks and Romans.

b. It is an artistic performance judged by a referee.

c. In some cases, a match can end in a stalemate.

d. It demands power and agility of body and mind.

Did You Know?

The motto of the World Chess Boxing Organization is "Fighting is done in the ring, and wars are waged (fought) on the board."

Inference 7. **Based on the present, what can be inferred about the future of chess boxing?**

a. The world will not accept chess boxing as a sport.

b. Chess boxing champions will continue to remain anonymous.

c. Chess boxing will continue to expand its following.

d. The world does not want to hear from champions anymore.

Summarizing Information

The sport of boxing is very old: The ancient Greeks fought ~~bare-gloved~~ *bareknuckle* boxing matches in their Olympic games while the Romans used leather gloves to protect themselves when boxing. The earliest form of chess, meanwhile, comes from India, where it was called *chaturanga*, meaning "four military people." These two sports are very different; one requires intellectual curiosity while the other requires physical strength. Chess boxing is a fragmented sport that demands both of these qualities from its competitors. Chess boxing was created by Iepe Rubingh, who got the idea for the sport from a copy of a chess boxing championship in a comic book. Rubingh competed in the sport's first professional exhibition in Amsterdam and later became the president of the World Chess Boxing Organization (WCBO). A chess boxing match is composed of 11 consecutive rounds of boxing and speed chess. If a chess match ends in a knockout, the winner is decided by the total number of technical points earned from the boxing phase. If the fighters are ahead on technical points, the fighter using the black pieces in chess is declared the winner. Since its conclusion, chess boxing has grown in popularity around the world.

B. Write a summary of the passage in your own words.

Vocabulary in Context

A. Complete the conversation below with vocabulary from the passage.

fortitude   storied   nimbleness   following   retired   level

A: I heard you've got tickets for the big fight.

B: Yeah, the media is calling it a _____¹ fight. I can't wait to see it!

A: So who do you think is going to win?

B: It's tough to say. The champ already _____² twice before this latest comeback. I don't know if he still has the _____³ to fight.

A: Well, he still has a great _____⁴. Most people have bet on him.

B: I think I would put my money on the newcomer.

A: Really? You'd choose inexperience over a _____⁵ career?

B: Yes, only because of his physical power and _____⁶.

B. Choose the sentences where the underlined words have the same meanings as they do in the passage.

1. a. The fisherman next to me had an <u>eclectic</u> collection of fish hooks.

    b. Professor Vick's <u>eclectic</u> style of teaching combines theory and practice.

2. a. The CEO accepted the <u>proposition</u> for a reduction in the workforce.

    b. Access to clean water is not a simple <u>proposition</u> for people living in that region.

3. a. A skilled politician, she used some <u>bareknuckle</u> tactics to get a majority of votes.

    b. The <u>bareknuckle</u> fight was bloody, resulting in a broken nose.

C. Complete the chart below by writing the phrasal verbs that match the definitions on the left. Then, write sentences using the phrasal verbs.

Definition	Phrasal Verb
1. to originate in	*come from*
2. to show that something is true	
3. to have been made at a certain time in the past	
4. to be equivalent or parallel	

1. *The tradition of competing in sports* **comes from** *the ancient Greek Olympic games.*

2. _____

3. _____

4. _____

Read the following excerpt from an interview by Lauren Wissot with Iepe Rubingh. Then, do the exercises.

🎧 16

Iepe Rubingh
on Chess Boxing

When asked what made chess boxing appealing to him:

"It's so sensual and pure in a way. If everything goes well, you're totally high. If not, you have to wrestle with the idea and find another way. With the fight, if you're able to dominate your opponent, you're euphoric. If not, you have to struggle to find another way to gain control. If his defenses are up, you have to take the fight to the body. You push your opponent; and in art, you have to push the idea as well. Being an artist, you have to be radical. Being a fighter, you have to be radical."

When asked about the relationship between chess and boxing:

"There really are differences. The sports truly are opposites in many ways. And I think the combination of the two sports adds something. Boxing adds something to chess, and chess adds something to boxing. You can compare it to American football. American football is like a game of chess. You've got all these coaches designing strategy, and then the quarterback begins to execute it physically. Chess boxing combines everything in one person."

When asked what it means to win or lose in a match of chess boxing:

"Well, if you lose against your opponent, you've lost in every aspect. I mean, if you're the better boxer and you couldn't get him down, and he checkmated you on the board, he's proved that he's not only strong enough to hold against you physically but also mentally capable enough to beat you on the chessboard. It makes the loss very brutal and complete at the same time."

Making Inferences
Check (✓) the statements that can be inferred from the above passage.

1. Being an artist has nothing in common with being a chess boxer. ☐
2. American football is like boxing because one person can do everything. ☐
3. Winning in chess boxing requires a combination of strategy and physical ability. ☐
4. Being dominated by an opponent makes a chess boxer feel euphoric. ☐
5. Chess boxing allows a competitor to defeat an opponent in every possible sense. ☐

Reflections   A chess boxing champion can be a capable boxer and perhaps even a decent chess player. But wouldn't it better to be a master of one sport rather than an average performer in a number of sports?

Selling Your Future on Wall Street

Unit Preview

A. Discuss the following questions.

1. Are college tuition fees high in your country? Which are the three most expensive universities?

2. In your country, do students pay their tuition fees with loans or with contributions from their parents? Which option is more common?

B. Write definitions in English for the following words and expressions. Check your definitions again after reading the passage to make sure they fit the context of the passage.

1. trajectory (*n.*)

2. default (*n.*)

3. deferment (*n.*)

4. forbearance (*n.*)

5. alleviate (*v.*)

6. roll out (*phr.*)

7. hand over (*phr.*)

8. stand to lose (*phr.*)

9. reimburse (*v.*)

10. bust (*n.*)

C. Based on the title "Selling Your Future on Wall Street," write down two topics that you expect to read about. Discuss your expectations. After reading the passage, check whether your expectations were met or not.

Reading Expectations	Were your expectations met?	
	Yes	No
1. *A new type of investment on Wall Street*		
2.		
3.		

Many students face financing dilemmas over tuition fees.

Higher education in the United States is extremely expensive. Average tuition costs at American colleges and universities are the highest in the world and have been on a steep upward trajectory for the past decade. To meet these ballooning educational costs, American students have been forced to take out ever higher amounts of student loans. In 2019, the total American student loan debt reached an alarming $1.6 trillion.

The good news is that student loans have made it possible for millions of students to earn higher education degrees. The repayment of the loans, however, is another story. Of the 44.7 million students who took out loans, 5.2 million ended up in default, 3.4 million in deferment, and 2.7 million in forbearance. Simply put, as of 2019, roughly 1 in 4 borrowers were unable to pay back their loans.

To alleviate the financial pain of student loans on college graduates, a number of education-related financial companies have rolled out a new model for paying for college. They are asking students to sell pieces of their future in exchange for college tuition loans. The arrangement is called an income-share agreement (ISA), and it works in a similar way to buying and selling shares in a company on Wall Street. Each student becomes, in a sense, an individual stock investment opportunity.

Students who sign ISAs agree to hand over to investors a percentage of their future earnings for a set period of time. The payback percentage is determined by a student's income; the higher the income, the higher the payback rate. If a student fails to find employment during the payback period, the company that issued the ISA stands to lose the entire investment as the student is not obligated to pay back a single dollar in case of unemployment.

 Q1

What percentage of borrowers are unable to pay back their student loans as of 2019?

 Q2

What do students get by signing an income-sharing agreement?

10

15

20

25

30

MIT, Cambridge, Massachusetts

Let's provide a concrete example for some clarity: Suppose that Student X needs $10,000 to complete her undergraduate degree in economics at University Y. If she took out a typical private bank loan of $10,000, she would have to pay back $146 a month for 10 years after her graduation—a total of $17,576. That would be almost twice the amount of the loan—a huge burden to Student X. But what if Student X decided to sell shares of her future income to Investment Company Z through an ISA?

40   Columbia University, New York City

Let's consider the following possible scenarios: Student X graduates and gets a job that pays the average starting salary for all economics majors who graduated from University Y: $47,000. At this salary, Student X would have to pay back Company Z a total of $15,673, which would be lower than the amount the student would have to pay for a private bank loan. However, if Student X were to get a $60,000-a-year job, she would have to reimburse $20,010 to Company Z. This amount would be higher than the private bank loan. There is also the possibility that the student remains unemployed for a number of years—or even for the entire payback period—in which case Company Z would collect less money than its investment in Student X or no money at all.

Q3
How can ISAs be beneficial to an educational-related financial lending company?

45

50

Selling one's future on Wall Street can be advantageous for a student as well as for the investment company that buys shares into the student's future. It can turn out to be very expensive for the student or a total bust for the investors. Like everything else on Wall Street, there are no guarantees.

55

◈ ETYMOLOGY: Words Associated with Wall Street ◈

stock: The word was used in the early 15th century English to mean "supply for future use" and in the mid-15th century to mean a "sum of money." It may be connected to the 14th-century usage of "money-box." The modern meaning of "subscribed capital of a corporation" dates back to the 1610s. *Example: Hours after announcing the merger, the company's stock shot up by more than 20%.*

company: The word has its origin in the Latin *companio*, literally meaning "bread fellow or eating mate." The Old French *compagnie* means "society" or "friendship." From the late 14th century, the English "company" had the meaning of "a number of people united to perform or carry out anything jointly," and it was later used in the commercial sense of "business association." The abbreviation "Co." dates back to the 1670s. *Example: A mid-sized company can employ over 1,000 workers.*

Reading Comprehension

Main Idea • **1. What is the passage mainly about?**

a. buying and selling tuition loans on Wall Street

b. making money by buying shares in students on Wall Street

c. a financial alternative to expensive tuition loans issued by U.S. banks

d. the rapidly rising costs of college tuition costs in the U.S.

> **Did You Know?**
>
> Private universities cost about twice as much as public universities in the U.S. In addition, students who attend public universities in their home state get a 50% discount.

Detail • **2. Which of the following facts is true?**

a. As of 2019, 44.7 million students were unable to pay their student loans.

b. In 2019, the total American student loan debt reached $1.6 billion.

c. 3.4 million students were in forbearance with their student loans as of 2019.

d. 5.2 million students defaulted on their student loans as of 2019.

Detail • **3. What happens if a student who signed an ISA remains unemployed during the payback period of a tuition loan after graduating from college?**

a. The student has to pay back the tuition loan in full.

b. The company that made the tuition loan loses its investment.

c. The company that made the tuition loan makes a huge profit.

d. The college that the student attended must repay the loan.

Vocabulary • **4. Which of the following verbs is different in meaning from the others?**

a. reapply   b. reimburse   c. repay   d. refund

Inference • **5. Which of the following is the ISA most similar to?**

a. getting a tuition scholarship   b. getting a loan from a bank

c. getting a job   d. buying or selling shares

Inference • **6. What does the passage suggest about ISAs?**

a. They are beneficial only to students.

b. They are beneficial only to lending companies.

c. They can be beneficial to students and lending companies.

d. They are always detrimental to students and lending companies.

Inference • **7. What can be inferred from the passage about college students in the U.S.?**

a. Millions have defaulted on their ISA payments.

b. Many have been forced to take out loans to pay for their expensive higher education.

c. Their total outstanding loan debt has been in steep decline.

d. 44.7 million students have sold shares in their future on Wall Street.

Summarizing Information

A. Find 10 mistakes in the summary of the passage. Then, correct them.

The total American student loan debt has been rising on a steep upward ~~scenario~~ *trajectory*, reaching an alarming $1.6

trillion in 2019. To meet these deflating educational costs, 44.7 million students have been forced to take out

loans. To increase the financial burden on students, some financial companies are offering a new way to pay for

college tuition. They are offering student loans in exchange for part of a student's future debt from a job. This is

called an income-share agreement (ISA), and it is similar to buying loans in a company on Wall Street. If students

who sign ISAs are able to get jobs, they must demand a certain percentage of their earnings to the financial

company; the higher the salary, the higher the payback amount. If the student remains employed during the

payback period, the financial company loses its entire investment. ISAs can be safe for students as well as lending

companies that buy shares in students' futures. ISAs can turn out to be very expensive for students or a total

success for lending financial companies. There are no losses on Wall Street.

B. Write a summary of the passage in your own words.

Vocabulary in Context

A. Complete the conversation below with vocabulary from the passage.

> scenario   ballooning   reimburse   stand to lose   steep

A: I've read that our university is planning to raise tuition costs again.

B: That would be a scary _____¹. The fees are already very high.

A: On top of that, dormitory fees have been _____² recently, too!

B: The seniors don't care, but freshmen _____³ the most.

A: That's so true. And since we're both freshmen, our costs will be very _____⁴.

B: We have to do something. Maybe we should join the student protests against the plan.

A: Yes. And we should demand that they _____⁵ us for any added costs!

B. Choose the sentences where the underlined words have the same meanings as they do in the passage.

1. a. The convenience store clerk moved more <u>stock</u> from the storage room to the shelves.

   b. The value of the new telecom company's <u>stock</u> shot up 100% in the last month.

2. a. The bank sent Gillian an email telling her she is now in financial <u>default</u>.

   b. If the browser does not work as fast, try using the <u>default</u> settings.

3. a. The <u>forbearance</u> period for the car loan was extended by a month.

   b. His wife's <u>forbearance</u> with his constant cheating has come to an end.

C. Complete the chart below by writing synonymous phrasal verbs that match the verbs on the left. Then, write sentences using the phrasal verbs.

Verb	Synonymous Phrasal Verb
1. introduce	*roll out*
2. surrender; yield	
3. repay	
4. obtain (an official service)	

1. *Plans to **roll out** the new self-driving car were postponed due to a software glitch.*

2. _____

3. _____

4. _____

Read the following passage about free higher education in the U.S. Then, do the exercises.

Free Higher Education
in the United States

🎧 18

   Despite having the highest college tuition costs in the world, the U.S. also provides opportunities for tuition-free higher education degrees. American students can get tuition-free education at small and large universities, military academies, and even prestigious universities such as MIT.

   A number of small colleges provide tuition-free education. The Curtis Institute of Music, located in Philadelphia, has a 4% acceptance rate and provides free tuition for all students. Students, however, must pay for their living expenses. Meanwhile, the Macaulay Honors College at City University of New York doesn't charge tuition to in-state students.

   The following military academies provide tuition-free education for all enrolled students: the U.S. Military Academy at West Point, the U.S. Coast Guard Academy, the U.S. Naval Academy, the U.S. Air Force Academy, and the U.S. Merchant Marine Academy. All living expenses, including room and board, are free. Students, however, must serve in the military for at least five years after graduation.

   The following top private American universities, among others, offer tuition-free education to selected students: MIT, in Massachusetts (8% acceptance rate), provides tuition-free education to students whose families earn under $90,000/year. Meanwhile, Stanford University, in California (11% acceptance rate), provides tuition-free education to students whose families earn under $60,000/year.

   The following Ivy League universities, among others, provide tuition-free education to selected students: Columbia University, in New York City (7% acceptance rate) provides tuition-free education to students whose families earn under $60,000/year. Similarly, Harvard University, in Massachusetts (5% acceptance rate) provides tuition-free education to students whose families earn under $60,000/year.

Making Inferences
Check (✓) the statements that can be inferred from the above passage.

1. The Curtis Institute of Music provides free tuition for selected students. ☐

2. The Macaulay Honors College provides free tuition to all its students. ☐

3. A free education provided by a military academy requires a military commitment. ☐

4. Some Ivy League Universities provide tuition-free education to some students. ☐

5. All American college students pay some of the highest tuition costs in the world. ☐

Reflections   A common argument against increasing higher education costs in the U.S. is that students from less affluent backgrounds cannot afford to attend prestigious universities, which have some of the highest costs in the world. However, all Ivy League universities, as well as other prestigious private and public universities, provide tuition-free education to students from less affluent families. Given these circumstances, does the argument still hold?

Passion and Profit in Numismatic Investments

Unit Preview

A. Discuss the following questions.

1. Which were the first minted coins in your country? What metals were they made of?

2. Are there any coins minted from gold or silver in your country?

B. Write definitions in English for the following words and expressions. Check your definitions again after reading the passage to make sure they fit the context of the passage.

1. intense (*adj.*)

2. handsome (*adj.*)

3. commemorative (*adj.*)

4. pile something into (*phr.*)

5. adage (*n.*)

6. govern (*v.*)

7. volatility (*n.*)

8. doctor (*v.*)

9. engrave (*v.*)

10. counterfeit (*v.*)

C. Based on the title "Passion and Profit in Numismatic Investments," write down two topics that you expect to read about. Discuss your expectations. After reading the passage, check whether your expectations were met or not.

Reading Expectations	Were your expectations met?	
	Yes	No
1. *Making money from investing in old coins*		
2.		
3.		

19

Unlike a normal coin collector, a numismatist has great knowledge about coins.

Collectors are a passionate bunch, and among them, numismatists are a particularly intense group when it comes to the object of their fascination: rare coins. For numismatists, the effort to accumulate available rare coins may be a financial investment, but it is not the only motivation. For them, the historical, cultural, and artistic values of coins and the preservation of their values are at least equally important. Still, numismatic investments can generate quite handsome profits.

Numismatists have several options for their rare coin investments. They can collect a country's regularly minted coins of different values and from different time periods; commemorative coins, which are coins issued for a limited period of time, honor a specific place, person, or event, and are not meant as currency; or error coins, which are coins that have some sort of minting mistake, and because of their rarity, they are more valuable than regularly minted coins. But before piling your money into any type of rare coin, it is useful to remember the adage "Buy the book before you buy the coin." That is, educate yourself to understand the investment you are about to make.

Rare coins are openly traded on the Internet. This virtual market for rare coins is governed by the same law of supply and demand that governs other free markets. This means there will be price volatility as well as price bubbles. No investor is protected from these basic market forces. Just as money can be easily made when a bubble is forming, money can be easily lost when the bubble bursts.

Consider the following example: In 2013, a 1995 U.S. Silver Eagle coin considered to be in "perfect condition" was sold for $86,654 at an auction.

Q1
What motivates numismatists to collect rare coins?

Q2
What does a proverb say about investing in rare coins?

15

20

25

30

Other 1995 Silver Eagle coins in great, but not perfect, condition had normally sold for about $4,000 each. Since the auction, however, over 200 other coins have received the "perfect condition" grade and now sell for about $20,000. The bubble has burst due to an increased market supply of perfect condition coins, and for the investor who paid $86,654 at auction in 2013, it means a $60,654 loss.

Investment-quality rare coins are generally certified by a professional coin-grading service such as the Professional Coin Grading Service (PCGS) or the Numismatic Guaranty Corporation (NGC). This certification eliminates the possibility that the coin is a fake and determines its relative value. Coins are graded on their condition and appearance with 70 grades ranging from "poor" to "perfect." Two coins that have the same grade and may appear identical, however, can still have subtle differences in appearance that will make one coin better—and thus more valuable—than the other.

Numismatic investors need to be aware of counterfeit and doctored coins. The Professional Numismatists Guild (PNG) defines coin doctoring as "the action of a person or the enabling of another to alter a coin's surface or appearance, usually to diminish or conceal defects, and thereby representing the condition or value of a coin as being superior to its actual condition or value." Examples of coin doctoring include using chemicals or lasers to hide scratches on the surface of a coin, engraving details, and altering dates and mint marks. Given that some rare coins sell for millions of dollars, there is great temptation to counterfeit or doctor rare coins. An expert should always be consulted before a large amount of money is invested in a rare coin.

Q3 Based on what criteria are coins graded by professional grading services?

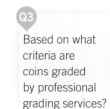

The first U.S. dollar coin, now valued at $10 million

A 2017 South African Krugerrand Gold coin

◆ **ETYMOLOGY: Words Associated with Coins** ◆

numismatic: The adjective is derived from the Greek *nomisma*, meaning "current coin" or "piece of money," and from the Latin *nummus*, meaning "coin." The meaning pertaining to "historical coins" comes from the late 16th-century French *numismatique*. The noun form, "numismatist," refers to a collector of historical coins. *Example: Numismatic coins are collectable because they are rare and are no longer produced. / Numismatists are typically avid readers of historical books.*

mint: The verb has its origins in the Latin *moneta*, which means "mint" or "coins." In Middle English, a "minter" was someone who "stamped coins to create money." From the 1540s, to "mint" has meant "to stamp metal to make coins." *Example: In some countries, coins are no longer minted.*

Reading Comprehension

Choose the best answers to the following questions on the passage "Passion and Profit in Numismatic Investments."

Main Idea 1. What is the passage mainly about?

a. bubbles and price volatility in numismatic investments

b. the motivations and risks of numismatic investments

c. procedures for investing in numismatics

d. types of numismatics available for investments

Detail 2. Which of the following is NOT considered a numismatic coin?

a. an error coin

b. a commemorative coin

c. a currently minted coin

d. a rare minted coin

Detail 3. According to the passage, which attribute of a coin is NOT important to numismatists?

a. its cultural significance

b. its artistic value

c. its gold content

d. its rarity

Detail 4. What is the distinguishing factor in two equally graded coins?

a. appearance   b. supply and demand   c. rarity   d. seller

Vocabulary 5. Which of the following verbs is different in meaning from the others?

a. fake   b. counterfeit   c. imitate   d. doctor

Inference 6. What does the passage suggest about altered rare coins?

a. They have inferior values to similar non-doctored coins.

b. Their appearances and surfaces have not been altered.

c. They are highly desired by collectors.

d. Alterations have been made to make their defects more visible.

Inference 7. What can be inferred from the passage about bubbles in the value of rare coins?

a. They are caused by the continuous minting of rare coins.

b. They can burst due to an oversupply of quality coins.

c. They can burst due to a decrease in the number available coins for sale.

d. They are created by high sales prices at auctions.

Summarizing Information

Numismatists, or collectors of rare coins, are particularly ~~concerned~~ *intense* about their coin-collecting efforts. For

numismatists, the ability to collect coins is as much financial as it is historical, cultural, and artistic. They can

collect printed coins, commemorative coins, and error coins. When investing in numismatic coins, one should

remember the mistake "Buy the book before you buy the coin." Because rare coins are openly traded on the

Internet, the law of supply and demand obeys this virtual market. Price fixing as well as price bubbles are

inevitable in this open trade. Price bubbles can burst due to an increased lack of rare coins on the market. Rare

coins are graded on their weight and appearance by professional coin-grading companies on a scale of 70 grades.

This certification eliminates the possibility that the coin is fake and determines its absolute value. As for fake coins,

numismatic investors need to be aware of counterfeit and pristine coins.

B. Write a summary of the passage in your own words.

Vocabulary in Context

A. Complete the conversation below with vocabulary from the passage.

numismatic   doctoring   minted   investment   bubble

A: So why exactly do you collect _____¹ coins?

B: To preserve their history. And I guess also as a financial _____².

A: This one looks ancient. When was it made?

B: It was _____³ during the rule of the Roman Emperor Hadrian.

A: Does it have any signs of _____⁴?

B: No, it's all original. And its value has gone up a lot in this financial

_____⁵ period.

B. Choose the sentences where the underlined words have the same meanings as they do in the passage.

1. a. My new job comes with a handsome yearly bonus.

   b. Clothes models are chosen for their handsome looks.

2. a. My neighbor piled a bunch of sticks on the ground to make a camp fire.

   b. He piled his life savings into a coffee shop, and now he's his own boss.

3. a. This year's sauvignon blanc has a subtle difference in dryness.

   b. Jimmy is a subtle liar; you never know when he is making stuff up.

C. Complete the chart below by writing the verb forms of the adjectives or nouns on the left. Then, write sentences using the verbs.

Adjective/Noun	Verb
1. commemorative	*commemorate*
2. engraving	
3. alteration	
4. governing	

1. *The purpose of Foundation Day is to* **commemorate** *the founding of the country.*

2. _____

3. _____

4. _____

Read the following passage that compares numismatic and bullion coins.
Then, do the exercises.

 20

Bullion Versus
Numismatics

Numismatic coins are rare or collectible coins. They can be made of gold, silver, or other metals such as nickel or copper. Bullion refers to precious metals such as gold, platinum, palladium, and silver. Bullion coins can therefore be made of gold, platinum, palladium, or silver and are purchased as investments or hedges against inflation. The intrinsic value of these precious metals is the same whether you purchase U.S. Gold Eagle coins, Canadian Gold Maple Leaf coins, U.S. Silver Eagle coins, Canadian Silver Maple Leaf coins, or South African Krugerrand gold coins. Their intrinsic value, however, fluctuates according to the market prices of the metals. Rare gold or silver coins, however, have an intrinsic value—the value of the precious metal—as well as a numismatic value, which is determined by the rarity and historical importance of the coin and can be many times the value of the precious metal content of that coin. A bullion coin's weight is expressed as an even amount, such as 1-ounce, 1/2-ounce, or even grams, and bullion coins are typically manufactured on a yearly basis. There is risk and potential profit in both bullion and numismatic investments. Commodity prices can fluctuate, raising or lowering the value of bullion coins. Similarly, the values of rare coins can rise and fall depending on the availability of coins on the market and the level of interest in them.

Making Inferences
Check (✓) the statements that can be inferred from the above passage.

1. Both numismatic and bullion coins can be purchased as financial investments. ☐

2. Numismatic coins can be made of different metals and are minted on a yearly basis. ☐

3. U.S. Silver Eagles and Canadian Gold Maple Leaf coins are rare and no longer minted. ☐

4. Bullion coins have intrinsic and numismatic values that fluctuate over time. ☐

5. Investing in numismatic or bullion coins does not guarantee a financial profit. ☐

Reflections   Societies are quickly moving toward electronic forms of financial transactions. Some countries are no longer minting or using coins. Is the collecting of coins as a form of investment no longer desirable due to this fact, or does this transition make coins even more desirable?

Chicago's Public Makeover: Art in the Loop

Unit Preview

A. Discuss the following questions.

    1. What are some well-known public artworks in your city?

    2. What is your favorite example of public art from around the world?

B. Write definitions in English for the following words and expressions. Check your definitions again after reading the passage to make sure they fit the context of the passage.

    1. congregate (*v.*)

    2. at the ready (*phr.*)

    3. train something on (*phr.*)

    4. pedigree (*n.*)

    5. adorn (*v.*)

    6. celestial (*adj.*)

    7. inlaid (*adj.*)

    8. burgeoning (*adj.*)

    9. trove (*n.*)

    10. in the loop (*phr.*)

C. Based on the title "Chicago's Public Makeover: Art in the Loop," write down two topics that you expect to read about. Discuss your expectations. After reading the passage, check whether your expectations were met or not.

Reading Expectations	Were your expectations met?	
	Yes	No
1. *Art in the city of Chicago*		
2.		
3.		

21

Q1

What is the current focus of visitors to the Loop neighborhood in the downtown area of Chicago?

The Loop is the recognized heart of downtown Chicago. This is where tourists congregate, armed with smartphones tethered on selfie sticks or high-powered DSLR cameras always at the ready to snap the perfect souvenir photo. And without a doubt, the Loop's historic architecture, river cruises, Chicago Riverwalk, and Millennium Park offer plenty to photograph. These days, however, visitors to the Loop prefer to train their cameras on public objects with an artistic pedigree—say, a Picasso, a Miro, a Chagall, or perhaps a Kapoor.

Heading the list of iconic public artwork on display at the Loop is a 50-foot, 160-ton sculpture made by Pablo Picasso and installed in the Daley Plaza. The unnamed art piece is known as *The Picasso* and has been described as an insect and a baboon, among other things. *The Picasso* was gifted in 1967 by its creator to the people of Chicago without any explanation as to what it might represent.

Joan Miró's mixed-media sculpture *The Sun, the Moon and One Star* adorns the Brunswick Building Plaza. *Miss Chicago*, as the statue is more popularly known today, is approximately 40 feet tall and is made of steel, wire mesh, concrete, bronze, and ceramic tile. The artwork represents a celestial female figure with a moon at her center and a star above her head.

Marc Chagall's *The Four Seasons* mosaic installation is composed of thousands of inlaid chips in over 250 colors. The artwork is displayed at Chase Tower Plaza, and it also contains pieces of native Chicago brick. The artwork depicts the four seasons, which, in the artist's words, represent "human life, both physical and spiritual, at its different ages." The mosaic contains scenes filled with birds, fish, flowers, suns, and pairs of lovers.

Perhaps the most recognizable of the Loop's public art pieces is *Cloud Gate*, a stainless-steel sculpture located in Millennium Park. Measuring 20 meters in length, 10 meters in height, and weighing a colossal 110 tons, British artist Anish Kapoor's *Cloud Gate* was inspired by mercury, and its highly polished surface recreates the look of a drop of the toxic liquid metal with faithful precision. The statue is also a physical gateway to Millennium Park.

These and other public artworks displayed in the Loop are only part

Joan Miró's *The Sun, the Moon and One Star*

of Chicago's burgeoning art collection, a trove of 500 paintings, statues, and murals displayed in 150 public places around the city ranging from police stations to municipal buildings. The collection's total insured value is over $85 million, with *Cloud Gate* alone valued at $23 million.

Chicago has had a long history of supporting public art. In 1978, it became the first U.S. city to create a city-funded public art program. The city's officials hoped that installed public art would bring value, meaning, and pride to Chicago. More recently, city officials declared 2017 "The Year of Public Art" and went the extra mile to announce a public art plan that included the expansion of resources to support the creation of public art throughout the city.

Investing in public art may be a wise thing for a city whose debt tops $45 billion. Chicago's public art makeover has brought an increasing number of visitors to the city and to the Loop in particular. Millennium Park is now the top tourist destination in the Midwest and among the top 10 in the U.S. Public art, it seems, has kept Chicago in the loop.

The Picasso in Chicago's Daley Plaza

45

Q2

Why did the city of Chicago's officials create a public art program?

50

Q3

How has Chicago's investment in public art paid off?

55

◆ **ETYMOLOGY: Words Associated with Art** ◆

mural: The word comes from the Latin words *muralis*, which means "of a wall," and *murus*, which means "wall." In the 15th century, the word "mural" was used as an adjective meaning "pertaining to a wall," and by 1915, it started being used in its present meaning as a noun, "painting on a wall." *Example: A number of forgotten murals were discovered during the restoration of the old church.*

mosaic: The word comes from the medieval Latin *musaicum*, meaning "mosaic work" or "work of the Muses," as medieval mosaics often depicted the Muses. The usage of the noun in English as "a piece of mosaic work" dates back to the 1690s. *Example: The cathedral was decorated with marble floors and columns as well as fine carvings and lively mosaics.*

Reading Comprehension

Choose the best answers to the following questions on the passage "Chicago's Public Makeover: Art in the Loop."

Main Idea • **1. What is the passage mainly about?**
   a. the Loop's long history of investing in public art
   b. major tourist attractions in Chicago
   c. historic attractions in the Loop
   d. Chicago's investment in public art in the Loop

Detail • **2. Which of the following statements is NOT true?**
   a. *The Picasso* has been described as a baboon and an insect.
   b. *Miss Chicago* is a 40-foot-tall celestial female figure.
   c. *The Four Seasons* is a mosaic installation at Chase Tower Plaza.
   d. *Cloud Gate* is a Millennium Park sculpture made of mercury.

Detail • **3. Which of the following numbers is associated with *Cloud Gate*?**
   a. $85 million   b. $23 million   c. 250   d. 40 feet

Vocabulary • **4. Which of the following words and phrases is different in meaning from the others?**
   a. art piece   b. object with artistic pedigree
   c. art collection   d. artwork

Detail • **5. Which of the following years is NOT connected with Chicago's public art?**
   a. 1967   b. 1976
   c. 1978   d. 2017

Inference • **6. What does the passage suggest about Chicago's public art?**
   a. It has all been installed in the Loop, the most visited area in Chicago.
   b. It has burdened the city with a debt that tops $45 billion.
   c. It has been a major factor in the increase in the local tourism industry.
   d. It has failed to bring meaning, value, and pride to Chicago.

Inference • **7. What can be inferred from the passage about Millennium Park?**
   a. It is less popular than the historical buildings in the Loop.
   b. It owes a lot of its popularity to Anish Kapoor's *Cloud Gate*.
   c. It is not very well known outside the city of Chicago.
   d. Visitors go there to snap pictures of *Cloud Gate*, *The Picasso*, and *Miss Chicago*.

Did You Know?

The lower 1.8 meters of the *Cloud Gate's* surface is wiped twice a day in order to remove fingerprints and other dirt. The entire sculpture is washed twice a year with 150 liters of liquid detergent and specialized cleaning equipment.

Did You Know?

The United Center arena, home of the NBA basketball team Chicago Bulls, displays a famous public artwork: a bronze statue of NBA legend Michael Jordan "in flight" toward the basket.

Summarizing Information

A. Find 10 mistakes in the summary of the passage. Then, correct them.

congregate

Tourists to Chicago ~~disappear~~ in its downtown area, known as the Loop. Here, they train their cameras on ordinary public artworks such as _The Picasso_, _Miss Chicago_, _The Four Seasons_, and _Cloud Gate_. Pablo Picasso gifted "The Picasso" to the people of Chicago without any explanation as to what it may adorn. _Miss Chicago_, a statue made of steel, wire mesh, concrete, bronze, and ceramic tile, represents a historical female figure. _The Four Seasons_ is a mosaic installation composed of thousands of microchips as well as pieces of native Chicago brick. _Cloud Gate_ is a statue that recreates the look of mercury with frightful precision. The public artworks in the Loop are a small part of Chicago's dwindling art collection: 500 paintings, statues, and murals displayed in 150 public places around the city. The city's art collection has a total admitted value topping $85 million with _Cloud Gate_ alone valued at $23 million. Chicago's public art hangover is bringing a growing number of visitors to the city. Public art is keeping Chicago in the dark.

B. Write a summary of the passage in your own words.

Vocabulary in Context

A. Complete the conversation below with vocabulary from the passage.

installation   snap   artwork   high-powered   makeover

A: Have you finished the preparations for your student art show?

B: Almost. I finally got a _____¹ camera to record it.

A: I guess you'll need someone to _____² photos at the opening of the show.

B: I will. I need pictures of the guests and of the _____³.

A: What kind of art are you showing, by the way?

B: The _____⁴ I made is a sculpture mixed with digital media.

A: Interesting. It will give the campus gallery a much-needed _____⁵.

B. Choose the sentences where the underlined words have the same meanings as they do in the passage.

1. a. The horses that she owns have obscure or unknown pedigrees.

   b. The buildings boast remarkable architectural pedigrees.

2. a. The models adorned the runway with a stunning display of spring fashion.

   b. The interior walls of the Palace of Versailles are adorned with masterful paintings.

3. a. Flags are always flown in front of City Hall and other municipal architectural works.

   b. The scientists agreed that it was a rarely seen municipal species of fish.

C. Complete the chart below by writing phrases that match the definitions on the left. Then, write sentences using the phrases.

Definition	Phrase
1. attached to	*tethered on*
2. prepared	
3. to aim something at another thing	
4. to make a special effort	

1. *The flag on a boat is usually **tethered on** a pole at the front.*

2. _____

3. _____

4. _____

Reading Connections

Read the following passage about graffiti street art. Then, do the exercises.

🎧 22

GRAFFITI AS STREET ART

This term "graffiti," derived from the Italian word *graffito*, meaning "to scratch," refers to the illegal act of spray-painting subway cars, buses, bridges, and buildings as well as other public or private areas. When not done for the purposes of vandalism, this form of street art is known as graffiti street art and has been carried out by countless unknown amateur artists as well as recognized street artists such as Jean-Michel Basquiat (1960-1988) and David Wojnarowicz (1954-1992), both of whom enjoyed mainstream commercial success. Artists who engage in graffiti street art are mostly freelancers; they do their graffiti work without a request from a sponsor. Their work is mostly illegal, as they do not usually have permission from public authorities or the owners of the spaces they choose for spray-painting. Graffiti street artwork therefore cannot be defined as public art, given the fact that public art is always sponsored by either a public (city, government, etc.) or a private (company, art investors, etc.) entity. Banksy is the most famous living graffiti street artist. This English artist has achieved international fame while remaining anonymous. His street artwork, such as *Kissing Coppers*, utilizes dark humor and irony to create powerful political and humanist messages with mass appeal. Like most other graffiti street art, Banksy's artwork is a response to the artist's social and political environment. Banksy and other graffiti artists aim to create artworks that contradict and challenge existing social conventions.

Making Inferences
Check (✓) the statements that can be inferred from the above passage.

1. Graffiti street art is a sponsored form of public art. ☐
2. The majority of graffiti street artists have enjoyed commercial success. ☐
3. Public art always has a sponsor, and this makes it different from graffiti street art. ☐
4. Banksy's artwork has achieved mass appeal thanks to its use of dark humor and irony. ☐
5. The purpose of graffiti street art is to fit within prevailing social contexts. ☐

Reflections Is it graffiti art or vandalism? Graffiti, by definition, is a form of vandalism since it is done without permission on another person's property. Would a museum allow its walls to be sprayed with graffiti? Would you consider graffiti sprayed on your house by a stranger artwork? What do you think?

LIFE**STYLE**

When Art Was a Revolution

design

Unit Preview

A. Discuss the following questions.

1. Who is you favorite artist? What is your favorite work of art?

2. Do you know which art movement your favorite artwork belongs to?

B. Write definitions in English for the following words and expressions. Check your definitions again after reading the passage to make sure they fit the context of the passage.

1. manifesto (*n.*) ....

2. scandalist (*n.*) ....

3. revel in (*phr.*) ....

4. bourgeoisie (*n.*) ....

5. urinal (*n.*) ....

6. anarchy (*n.*) ....

7. indignantly (*adv.*) ....

8. flush down (*phr.*) ....

9. propagandist (*n.*) ....

10. imbecility (*n.*) ....

C. Based on the title "When Art Was a Revolution," write down two topics that you expect to read about. Discuss your expectations. After reading the passage, check whether your expectations were met or not.

Reading Expectations	Were your expectations met?	
	Yes	No
1. *A particular movement in art*		
2.		
3.		

Q1

What was the intention of the Dadaists regarding the arts?

If Dada were to be called an art movement, it would be extremely difficult to define its aesthetic. The reason is that Dada called for the absolute abolishment of all forms of art: "No more painters, no more writers, no more musicians… nothing, nothing, nothing" (from Tristan Tzara's *Dada Manifesto*). The Dadaists—the practitioners of Dada—were skillful scandalists who reveled in antagonizing the fine-arts establishment and the bourgeoisie that supported it. Dadaists replaced oil paintings with artwork made of everyday materials, photographs with pictures of cut-up newspaper clippings, and sculptures of human bodies with urinals. If Dada was art, then art was a revolution.

Dada started out against the backdrop of World War I, arguably the most brutal and atrocious of all modern conflicts. The artists that took part in the Dada revolution—Tristan Tzara, Hugo Ball, Jean Arp, Hannah Höch, Man Ray, Marcel Duchamp, and Raoul Hausmann, among others—crafted their artistic responses as protests against the inhumanity of the war and the societies that were engaged in that horrific conflict. Originally intended as a political movement, Dada essentially became a form of antiauthoritarian artistic anarchy.

The Dadaists were poets, pioneers of performance art, and intermedia artists. Their creations were intended to shock audiences. Marcel Duchamp submitted his famous urinal as a piece of art to the Society of Independent Artists that he had helped found, and when his submission was rejected on the basis of not being a "piece of art," he indignantly resigned from the society. That moment in 1917 changed art forever. From that point on, the value and definition of an artwork was no longer dependent on its content or appearance but rather on the purpose for which it was created. And the purpose for Duchamp's urinal was precisely to flush down any pre-existing concepts of art.

Dada was born in 1916 at the Cabaret Voltaire, a venue for satirical shows opened by German writer Hugo Ball in Zurich, Switzerland, where he had taken refuge from World War I.

Marcel Duchamp's urinal, titled *Fountain*

Q2

Why did Marcel Duchamp submit his famous urinal as a piece of art?

Group photograph of Dada artists in 1920, Paris

The cabaret, named after the 18th-century French satirist, staged masked plays and modern dances as well as poetry readings. The reading of the nonsensical poem *Karawane* by Hugo Ball on August 15, 1916, marked the beginning of Dada. World War I ended in 1918, but Dadaists were just getting started in their fight against the establishment.

Dada's chief propagandist, Romanian-born Tristan Tzara, read his provocative manifestos during Dadaist meetings and performances staged in places such as the Cabaret Voltaire. Tzara called these performances "explosions of elective imbecility" to emphasize that any attempt at creating art was futile. In his *Dada Manifesto*, Tzara described Dada as "an abolition of memory, of archaeology, of prophets, of the future, and of every god that is the immediate product of spontaneity." Dada would do to the arts what the war had done to humanity.

Q3
Why did Tzara call the Dada performances "explosions of elective imbecility"?

Dada's anarchist spirit spread from Berlin to Paris, New York, and even Tokyo. Dada would die out in Paris in the early 1920s due to in-fighting between Tzara and poet André Breton. By that time, Breton was already at work on the next avant-garde idea, Surrealism. "Dada," said Breton, "very fortunately, is no longer an issue and its funeral, about May 1921, caused no rioting." Dada may have died in 1921, but it lives on through the many art movements it inspired: abstract and conceptual art, performance art, pop, and installation art. As a Dadaist might say, "Dada is dead. Long live Dada!"

Eröffnung der ersten großen Dada-Ausstellung
in den Räumen der Kunsthandlung Dr. Burchard, Berlin, am 5. Juni 1920.
Von links nach rechts: Hausmann, Hanna Höch, Dr. Burchard, Baader, W. Herzfelde, dessen Frau, Dr. Oz, George Grosz, John Heartfield.

Grand opening of the first Dada exhibition: International Dada Fair, Berlin, 1920

◆ **ETYMOLOGY: Words Associated with Dada** ◆

revolution: The word comes from the late Latin *revolutionem*, meaning "a revolving." The late 14th-century *revolucion* means a "course or revolution of celestial bodies (stars, planets)." In the 15th century, the French word acquired the sense of "instance of great change in affairs." The English word "revolution" was derived from French and took the political meaning of "the overthrowing of an established political system" around 1600. *Example: The global population has increased dramatically since the Industrial Revolution.*

establishment: The word was used with the meaning of "settled arrangement" in the 15th century and comes from *establish + -ment*. In 1731, the word was used with the meaning of "established church." The meaning of "a place of business" dates back to 1832. The current meaning of "a social matrix of ruling people and institutions" has been used since 1923. *Example: The establishment in Washington is making extensive use of the media to hold on to its power and influence.*

Reading Comprehension

Main Idea

1. What is the passage mainly about?
   a. the membership and following of Dada
   b. the history and aims of Dada
   c. the intentions and methods of Dadaists
   d. the fall and aftermath of Dada

Detail

2. Which of the following groups can be categorized as Dadaists?
   a. established writers   b. the bourgeoisie
   c. authorities   d. scandalists

Detail

3. Which of the following quotes is NOT an accurate description of Dada?
   a. "a protest with the fists against art"
   b. "a destruction of memory and the future"
   c. "an abolition of artistic anarchy"
   d. "nothing, nothing, nothing"

Detail

4. Which of the following Dada artists is credited with starting the movement?
   a. Hugo Ball   b. Marcel Duchamp
   c. Tristan Tzara   d. André Breton

Vocabulary

5. Which of the following words is different in meaning from the others?
   a. anarchy   b. revolution   c. uprising   d. riot

Inference

6. What does the passage suggest about Dadaists?
   a. They did not call for violent means of bringing changes in the arts.
   b. They were interested in preserving established conventions in the arts.
   c. They pioneered fields of art such as intermedia and performance art.
   d. Their creations were always intelligible and rational.

Inference

7. What can be inferred from the passage about Dada?
   a. Its followers and critics understood its aesthetic very easily.
   b. It was a response to the inhumanity of World War I.
   c. It was originally intended as an artistic form of anarchy.
   d. Its influence ended with its demise in 1921.

Did You Know?

Dada got its name when Richard Huelsenbeck, a German artist living in Zurich, and Hugo Ball came upon the word in a French-German dictionary. "Dada" is "yes, yes" in Romanian, "rocking horse" in French," and a sign of foolish innocence in German.

Did You Know?

The Cabaret Voltaire was located very close to the apartment of Vladimir Ilyich Lenin, the soon-to-be Premier of the Soviet Union, who spent a year (1917) in exile with his wife in Zurich.

Summarizing Information

A. Find 10 mistakes in the summary of the passage. Then, correct them.

abolishment
Dada was a revolutionary art movement that called for the complete ~~restructuring~~ of all forms of established art. It started out against the backdrop of World War I, the most brutal and benign of all modern conflicts. Tristan Tzara and other Dadaists reveled in admiring the fine-arts establishment and the bourgeoisie that supported it. Dada artists performed shocking reading performances and created artworks such as urinals. If Dada was art, then art was a composition. The purpose for artwork such as Duchamp's urinal was to eliminate any pre-existing piece of art. Dada started out in Zurich at the Cabaret Voltaire in 1916 with the reading of the lyrical poem *Karawane* by Hugo Ball. Tristan Tzara, Dada's chief opponent, read his provocative manifestos in places such as the Cabaret Voltaire. Tzara called such readings "explosions of elective ingenuity" to emphasize that any attempt at creating art was useless. In his *Dada Manifesto*, Tzara called "an emergence of memory, of archaeology, of prophets, of the future, and of every god that is the immediate product of spontaneity." Dada practically ended 1921, but it prevented art movements such as abstract and conceptual art, performance art, pop, and installation art.

B. Write a summary of the passage in your own words.

Vocabulary in Context

A. Complete the conversation below with vocabulary from the passage.

flushed down   scandalist   revels in   manifesto   indignantly   urinal

A: So are you voting for Timmy for student body leader?

B: Timmy? He's such a _____¹. He loves to antagonize people.

A: I think he would respond _____² to being called that.

B: But it's true, isn't it? He just _____³ making people angry.

A: That's his strategy: make fun of some students to get the support of others.

B: That's true. His last speech sounded like a Dadaist _____⁴.

A: I'm surprised he didn't bring Duchamp's _____⁵.

B: I wish he had. I would've _____⁶ his speech in it.

B. Choose the sentences where the underlined words have the same meanings as they do in the passage.

1. a. Burger Supreme announced that the underlined establishment would drop onion rings from the menu.

   b. The literary establishment welcomed the new fantasy novel with rave reviews.

2. a. Human trafficking is an atrocious crime that takes place globally.

   b. Doctors have a reputation for atrocious handwriting.

3. a. The shorter boxer prefers the in-fighting style as he constantly pushes his opponent against the ropes.

   b. This political in-fighting is threatening to break the party apart.

C. Complete the chart below by writing the noun forms of the adjectives on the left. Then, write sentences using the nouns.

Adjective	Noun
1. satirical	*satire*
2. nonsensical	
3. atrocious	
4. brutal	

1. *His new novel is basically a fictional political* **satire** *with a sprinkling of realism.*

2. _____

3. _____

4. _____

Reading Connections

Read the following passage about the making of a Dadaist poem. Then, do the exercises.

🎧 24

How to *Make* a **Dadaist** Poem

If Dada were to succeed in its aim to undermine the fundamental structures of a rational, ordered society, then it had to start by undermining language itself. In order to challenge the conventional use of language in poetry, Tristan Tzara proposed the freeing of text from its accepted conventions: spelling, grammar, punctuation, and rationality. Here is Tzara's recipe for a Dada poem:

Take a newspaper / Take a pair of scissors / Choose an article as long as you are planning to make your poem / Cut out the article / Cut out each of the words that make up this article and put them in a bag / Shake it gently / Take out the scraps one after the other, in the order in which they left the bag / Copy conscientiously / The poem will be like you / And here you are, a writer, infinitely original, with a sensibility that is charming, though beyond the understanding of the vulgar.

Tzara does not suggest that Dadaists should really write poems this way. He is suggesting that the Dadaist writer needs to be original in a way the "vulgar" masses cannot understand. And here the masses symbolize the establishment, the conventional. Hugo Ball's poem *Karawane* fits perfectly Tzara's definition of original as well as the overall intention of Dada. Here are the opening lines of this nonsensical poem aimed at undermining the very foundations of language:

jolifanto bambla o falli bambla
großiga m'pfa habla horem
egiga goramen
higo bloiko russula huju
hollaka hollala

Making Inferences
Check (✓) the statements that can be inferred from the above passage.

1. Tristan Tzara called for the abandonment of all conventions in the use of language. ☐

2. Tzara wanted to replace randomness with rationality. ☐

3. In Tzara's opinion, a Dadaist poem should resemble a lottery drawing. ☐

4. *Karawane* is completely incomprehensible in any language. ☐

5. Tzara used the term "vulgar" to describe Dadaist poets. ☐

Reflections   Ancient Greek philosopher Socrates once compared children to Dadaists: "The children now love luxury, have bad manners, contempt for authority; they show disrespect for elders and love chatter in place of exercise. They contradict their parents and tyrannize their teachers." Have children always been Dadaists in the eyes of adults?

The Making of a Dalai Lama

Unit Preview

A. Discuss the following questions.

1. Do you know roughly what percentage of your country's population practices Buddhism?

2. Do you know the names of some of the Buddhist orders (schools) in your country?

B. Write definitions in English for the following words and expressions. Check your definitions again after reading the passage to make sure they fit the context of the passage.

1. autonomous (*adj.*) ....

2. plateau (*n.*) ....

3. revered (*adj.*) ....

4. embody (*v.*) ....

5. exile (*n.*) ....

6. reincarnation (*n.*) ....

7. meticulous (*adj.*) ....

8. assert (*v.*) ....

9. octogenarian (*n.*) ....

10. (high) stakes (*n.*) ....

C. Based on the title "The Making of a Dalai Lama," write down two topics that you expect to read about. Discuss your expectations. After reading the passage, check whether your expectations were met or not.

Reading Expectations	Were your expectations met?	
	Yes	No
1. *Tibetan Buddhism*		
2.		
3.		

Tibet is known as "the roof of the world." The territory of this region of China, officially named the Tibet Autonomous Region, occupies a vast area of high plateaus and mountains in Central Asia, including Mount Everest.

5 Throughout the centuries, Tibet has maintained a unique culture, language, and religion. At the center of Tibetan life is a highly revered person who embodies the very spirit of Tibetan values and religious tradition: the Dalai Lama, the spiritual and political leader of the approximately 6.5 million Tibetan people.

10 Tibetan Buddhism is a religion in exile, as is its leader, the 14th Dalai Lama. The Dalai Lama was forced to leave his residence—the Potala Palace in Lhasa, the capital of Tibet—when the Chinese occupied Tibet in 1959. The Dalai Lama now lives in exile in Dharamshala, India, together with the Central Tibetan Administration, which is the Tibetan government in exile.

15 In Tibetan Buddhism, the Dalai Lama is a reincarnation of a past lama who decided to be reborn again to continue his important work. *Dalai* is a Mongol word that means "ocean," in reference to the depth of the Dalai Lama's wisdom. A *lama* is a Buddhist teacher that can be a monk, a nun, or even a common person. The current Dalai Lama, Tenzin Gyatso, was born in

20 1935 in Amdo, Tibet, and is the 14th reincarnation of the Dalai Lama. The first Dalai Lama was Gedun Drupa (1391-1474), but he was given this revered title posthumously as it was only applied from the third reincarnation of the Dalai Lama: Sonam Gyatso.

In Tibetan tradition, when a Dalai Lama passes away, the High Lamas of

25 the Gelugpa Tradition and the Tibetan government are tasked with finding his reincarnation: a boy who is born at the time of the passing away of the Dalai Lama. This is a very meticulous and complicated process that can take a number of years to be completed. For example, it took four years for the current Dalai Lama to be found.

Q1
Where does the leader of the approximately 6.5 million Tibetans live?

Q2
Who must locate a future reincarnation of a Dalai Lama?

The Potala Palace in Lhasa, Tibet

Philoso

The High Lamas look for the Dalai Lama's reincarnation in a number of ways: One of the High Lamas may have a dream about a mark or location that will identify the boy, or the High Lamas may go to Lhamo Latso, a holy lake located in central Tibet, to seek a sign from the lake. Once the boy has been located, he is shown a number of objects, some of which belonged to the Dalai Lama. If the boy correctly chooses the objects that belonged to the Dalai Lama, this is seen as a sign that the boy is the reincarnation of the Dalai Lama.

The 14th Dalai Lama in prayer on a throne

So far, the searches for the Dalai Lama have been limited to Tibet even though the third Dalai Lama was born in Mongolia. The next search, however, will be extremely problematic as Tibet is no longer independent, and the ruling Chinese communist government is not interested in finding the true reincarnation of the current Dalai Lama, a figure it naturally opposes. Essentially, the Chinese would only approve of a Dalai Lama who would be loyal to the Communist Party.

45

Why is the search for the next Dalai Lama problematic?

Knowing this, the current Dalai Lama has asserted that he will not be reborn in a place that is not free. That would rule out the Tibet Autonomous Region, which, despite its name, is not a self-governing state. More importantly perhaps, the octogenarian Tenzin Gyatso has hinted that he may not choose to be reborn. That would prevent the Chinese from appointing a false Dalai Lama who would only serve to advance their political goals. The spiritual stakes are very high in the roof of the world.

50

55

◆ ETYMOLOGY: Words Associated with Buddhism ◆

religion: The word originates from the Latin *religionem*, meaning "respect for what is sacred, reverence for the gods; conscientiousness, a sense of right, moral obligation; fear of the gods; divine service, holiness." In Old French, the word *religion* means "piety, devotion; religious community." In 14th-century English, *religion* had the meaning of a "particular system of faith," which is maintained today. *Example: Buddhism is the world's fourth largest religion with over 500 million followers.*

spiritual: The word comes from the Latin *spiritus*, meaning "of breathing, of the spirit." The Old French word *spirituel* and Middle English *spiritual* mean "of or concerning the church." The modern sense refers to "related to the human spirit or soul." *Example: After he donated all of his money to charity, his only interest became his spiritual life.*

Reading Comprehension

Main Idea 1. **What is the passage mainly about?**

a. the traditions, role, and election process of the Dalai Lama

b. the history of Tenzin Gyatso, the Dalai Lama

c. Tibet and Tibetan Buddhism

d. the search for a new Dalai Lama

Did You Know?

Tibetan Buddhism is a form of Buddhism practiced in Tibet, Bhutan, Chinese Central Asia, the southern Siberian regions, and Mongolia.

Detail 2. **What is the literal meaning of "Dalai Lama"?**

a. a most revered person

b. a reincarnation of a monk

c. a High Lama of the Gelugpa Tradition

d. a Buddhist teacher of great wisdom

Detail 3. **Which of the following is NOT true about Tibet?**

a. It has a unique language, culture, and religion.

b. It is called "the roof of the world."

c. Its present spiritual leader is the 14th Dalai Lama.

d. It is an independent state in Central Asia.

Did You Know?

A bill introduced in the U.S. Congress would call for sanctions on any Chinese official who interferes with Tibetan Buddhist succession practices.

Detail 4. **Who was the first Dalai Lama?**

a. Sonam Gyatso

b. Tenzin Gyatso

c. Gedun Drupa

d. Lhamo Latso

Vocabulary 5. **Which of the following adjectives is different in meaning from the others?**

a. ruling

b. autonomous

c. self-governing

d. independent

Inference 6. **What does the passage suggest about the 14th Dalai Lama?**

a. He has already determined the location of his next reincarnation.

b. He has the ability to choose whether and where he will reincarnate.

c. He is hopeful that the Chinese will be able to locate his next reincarnation.

d. He is willing to reincarnate in an occupied Tibet.

Inference 7. **What can be inferred from the passage about Tibetan Buddhism?**

a. It requires the mandatory reincarnation of a Dalai Lama.

b. It embraces the principle of reincarnation.

c. It insists that the Dalai Lama be loyal to the Chinese Communist Party.

d. It recommends that the Dalai Lama come from the High Lamas of the Gelugpa Tradition.

Summarizing Information

A. Find 10 mistakes in the summary of the passage. Then, correct them.

Tibet, officially named the Tibet Autonomous Region, is an area of high *plateaus* ~~valleys~~ and mountains in Central Asia whose people have maintained a unique culture, language, and religion. The Dalai Lama is the economic and political leader of the roughly 6.5 million Tibetan people. The 14th Dalai Lama is a leader in return. He was willing to leave the capital of Tibet when the Chinese occupied Tibet in 1959. The Dalai Lama is a manifestation of a past lama, according to Tibetan Buddhism. When a Dalai Lama passes away, the High Lamas of the Gelugpa Tradition are obsessed with finding his reincarnation. This current and complicated process can take a few years to be completed. Though searches for the Dalai Lama have been limited to Tibet, the next search will be successful as Tibet is no longer independent. The ruling Chinese communist government is not interested in finding the true reincarnation of the Dalai Lama and would only approve of a Dalai Lama who would be opposed to the Communist Party. Knowing this, Tenzin Gyatso has hinted that he may not be reborn. This would allow the Chinese from appointing a false Dalai Lama.

B. Write a summary of the passage in your own words.

Vocabulary in Context

A. Complete the conversation below with vocabulary from the passage.

posthumously   nuns   monks   religions   revered

A: You're back from your vacation in England, Becky. How was it?

B: Very, hmmm... historical. I saw a lot of palaces, cathedrals, and monasteries.

A: Did you see any _____¹ or _____² living there?

B: No, but I did see the skulls and bones of many _____³ saints.

A: Do you have a favorite saint? My favorite saint has to be St. Nicholas of Bari.

B: I've heard that he was made a saint _____⁴.

A: That's right. And centuries after his death, he became one of the most popular saints in the Catholic and Orthodox _____⁵.

B. Choose the sentences where the underlined words have the same meanings as they do in the passage.

1. a. The federation was divided into several autonomous republics.

b. The race is on for the development of autonomous driving cars.

2. a. Under new management, the former burger diner was reborn as a fancy restaurant.

b. She wishes to be reborn as a movie star in a future life.

3. a. Physical music sales figures were higher than digital download revenue in 2017.

b. There are powerful political figures standing in the way of justice.

C. Complete the chart below by writing the adjective forms of the words on the left. Then, write sentences using the adjectives.

Word	Adjective
1. problem	*problematic*
2. posthumously	
3. assert	
4. oppose	

1. *Alcohol becomes **problematic** when it interferes with your daily life.*

2. _____

3. _____

4. _____

Reading Connections

Read the following passage about the 14th Dalai Lama. Then, do the exercises.

THE FOURTEENTH DALAI LAMA

🎧 26

Tenzin Gyatso, the 14th Dalai Lama of Tibetan Buddhism, was born with the name of Lhamo Thondup on July 6, 1935, in the province of Amdo in northeastern Tibet. The High Lamas of the Gelugpa Tradition had been searching for the next reincarnation of the 13th Dalai Lama for many years. A number of signs brought them to the young Lhamo Thondup.

The first sign occurred when the face of the embalmed 13th Dalai Lama mysteriously turned northeast. Shortly afterward, a High Lama had a vision of Amdo when looking in the sacred lake Lhamo Latso. The vision showed a three-story monastery with a gold and turquoise roof, and another vision showed a small house with strange gutters. The monastery at Kumbum in Amdo fit the description, and the house of the three-year-old Lhamo Thondup was soon identified. The High Lamas performed the object identification test next. They gave the boy a number of objects that included a rosary and a bell that had belonged to the deceased 13th Dalai Lama. The boy instantly identified the items, shouting, "It's mine. It's mine!"

At the age of five, Lhamo began his Buddhist training with the high monks at Lhasa, Tibet's capital, at what was his official residence at that time. The young Lhamo Thondup was renamed Jamphel Ngawang Lobsang Yeshe Tenzin Gyatso and given leadership of Tibet, which had become a Chinese province in 1950. In March 1959, Tibetans demanded an end to Chinese rule, but the Chinese army crushed the revolt by killing thousands. Fearing that the Chinese government would also kill him, the Dalai Lama fled from Tibet to India with thousands of followers. The Indian prime minister, Jawaharlal Nehru, allowed the 14th Dalai Lama to form the Tibetan Government in Exile in Dharamshala, India, where the Dalai Lama still lives today.

Making Inferences
Check (✓) the statements that can be inferred from the above passage.

1. The current Dalai Lama is a reincarnation of the 13th Dalai Lama.   ☐
2. Lhamo Thondup's embalmed face mysteriously turned northeast.   ☐
3. The young Tenzin Gyatso successfully passed the object identification test.   ☐
4. The 14th Dalai Lama continues to rule Tibet with the help of the Chinese.   ☐
5. The Indian people welcomed the Dalai Lama in their country.   ☐

Reflections   According to a study conducted by the Pew Research Center, more than 80 countries endorse a specific religion, either as an official, government-endorsed religion or by extending one religion preferential treatment over other religions. On the other hand, 10 countries are hostile to religion in general. Should governments either promote, endorse, or regulate religion?

Newcomb's Dilemma:
Is Free Will Really Free?

Unit Preview

A. Discuss the following questions.

1. Do you believe that things happen randomly or for a reason?

2. Do you believe that your choices in life are your own, or were they made by a higher power?

B. Write definitions in English for the following words and expressions. Check your definitions again after reading the passage to make sure they fit the context of the passage.

1. determinism (*n.*) _____

2. split (*adj.*) _____

3. favor (*v.*) _____

4. real-life (*adj.*) _____

5. implication (*n.*) _____

6. damnation (*n.*) _____

7. salvation (*n.*) _____

8. analogy (*n.*) _____

9. predisposition (*n.*) _____

10. trigger (*v.*) _____

C. Based on the title "Newcomb's Dilemma: Is Free Will Really Free?" write down two topics that you expect to read about. Discuss your expectations. After reading the passage, check whether your expectations were met or not.

Reading Expectations	Were your expectations met?	
	Yes	No
1. *The ability to make one's own choices*		
2.		
3.		

Q1

What philosophical question is Newcomb's Problem based on?

Newcomb's Dilemma is at the core of a philosophical problem named after William A. Newcomb, the American theoretical physicist who thought it up in 1960. This is essentially the age-old question of free will versus determinism: Do you believe people are making their own choices when selecting books to read from a library, or were there forces greater than their understanding that brought them to making those selections? Read Newcomb's Problem and make your own decision:

Two closed boxes, A and B, are placed on a table. Box A contains $1,000. Box B is either empty or contains $1 million. You do not know which. You have two choices: 1. Take both boxes; 2. Take Box B only. You can keep the contents of the box or boxes you take, and your aim is to get the most money. It is a piece of cake, right?

Is free will or determinism correct?

Not quite. The box test was set by a super-intelligent being who has already predicted your choice. If the being predicted that you would take both boxes, it left Box B empty. In addition, if the being predicted that you would make a random choice by tossing a coin, it left Box B empty. On the other hand, if the being predicted that you would only take Box B, it put $1 million in it. Would you choose both boxes or Box B alone?

Before you make your selection, it is important to know what others chose. When Newcomb's Problem was presented in the magazine *Scientific American* in 1973, about 70% of the readers chose to take Box B. In a more recent mass survey on Newcomb's Problem, the results were much closer: 55% chose Box B, and 45% chose both boxes. Other surveys returned similar results: a split opinion slightly favoring the Box B solution. But what does your choice mean?

If you believe that the super-intelligent being has already determined your fate, the only way you can get the $1 million is by choosing Box B. On the other hand, by choosing both boxes, you believe that no super-intelligent being can know or determine your future choices. In other

Q2

What have surveys conducted on Newcomb's Problem shown?

words, your free will cannot be predetermined. More respondents, though by a small margin, believe in determinism, or the ability of the super-intelligent being to predetermine the outcome. But are there real-life implications associated with their response? The answer is yes, and they can range from religion to health.

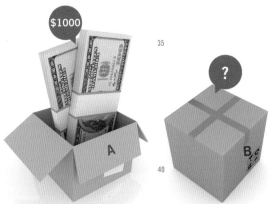

Newcomb's Problem illustrated

Let's consider the example of Calvinism, a Christian belief system proposed by John Calvin in the 16th century. Calvin asserted that all humans, regardless of their actions, are predetermined by God to either eternal damnation or salvation. God made the choice already, and people can do nothing to change their destiny. So a person can live without sin, putting faith in God's decision for his or her fate. This is similar to choosing Box B. Or a person can live a life of sin, knowing that it would not change his or her fate anyway. This is similar to choosing both boxes. This is a daily choice we must all make.

Or we can consider a more scientific real-life analogy to Newcomb's Problem. Diabetes is known to be caused by a genetic predisposition. People predisposed to diabetes should not eat too much sugar as this may trigger the disease. Again, we are back to Newcomb's boxes. Box B would be: Believe in what your genetic predisposition tells you and keep away from cookies. Both boxes: Who knows for sure if science is right? There may be other factors contributing to diabetes. Eat all the cookies you want! Which brings us back to Newcomb's Dilemma: Free will or follow your destiny? It is time to make your choice.

Q3
What are some real-life implications of Newcomb's Problem?

◈ **ETYMOLOGY: Words Associated with Determinism** ◈

sin: The word originates in the Latin word *sons*, meaning "guilty or criminal." From the Latin, we get the Dutch *zoned* and German *Sünde*, meaning "sin, transgression, trespass, or offense." The Old English *synn* means "moral wrongdoing, injury, mischief, enmity, feud, guilt, crime, offense against God, or misdeed." The spelling was changed in modern English, but some of the Old English meanings were preserved. *Example: Greed is one of the seven deadly sins listed in the Bible.*

fate: The word originates from the Latin *fatum*, meaning "a prophetic declaration of what must be or a prediction." In Old French, *fate* means "one's lot or destiny." The meaning of "that which must be" dates back to Middle English. The Old French and Middle English meanings have been retained in modern usage. *Example: He believed it was his fate to become a soldier, as his father and grandfather before him.*

Reading Comprehension

Choose the best answers to the following questions on the passage "Newcomb's Dilemma: Is Free Will Really Free?"

Main Idea

1. What is the passage mainly about?
   a. the philosophical problem of determinism
   b. the philosophical problem of free will
   c. the choice between free will and determinism
   d. the life and theories of William A. Newcomb

Detail

2. What would the super-intelligent being do if it predicted one would choose Box B?
   a. It would leave it empty.
   b. It would place $1,000 in it.
   c. It would make a random choice.
   d. It would place $1 million in it.

Detail

3. Which of the following is true about choosing both boxes in Newcomb's test?
   a. One believes that determinism has lead him or her to making the choice.
   b. One believes that his or her free will cannot be predetermined.
   c. One believes in a super-intelligent being.
   d. One believes that he or she has no control over any personal choices.

Detail

4. What is the maximum amount of money that can be won in Newcomb's test?
   a. $1,000,000   b. $1,001,000   c. $1,000,001   d. $1,100,000

Vocabulary

5. Which of the following is different in meaning from the others?
   a. predestination   b. predisposition   c. destiny   d. fate

Inference

6. What does the passage suggest about Calvinism?
   a. It proposes that people can live with sin by putting their faith in God.
   b. It is a Christian belief system based on human free will.
   c. It asserts that all human action is predetermined by God.
   d. It encourages people to choose both boxes in Newcomb's test.

Inference

7. What can be inferred from the passage about diabetes?
   a. People predisposed to diabetes are advised to eat lots of sugar.
   b. It is a real-life analogy to Newcomb's Problem.
   c. It is not believed to be caused by a genetic predisposition.
   d. Sugar intake is the only triggering factor of the disease.

Summarizing Information

determinism

Newcomb's Problem is essentially a question of free will versus ~~existentialism~~. This philosophical test involves

making a difference between two closed boxes, A and B, the first containing $1,000 and the second being either

empty or containing $1 million. The test also involves the decision of a super-intelligent being, who has already

taken the test taker's choice. In recent surveys, a majority of people found Box B. This suggests that they believed

in a super-intelligent being's ability to change the outcome of the test. A slightly lesser number of people chose

both boxes, believing in free choice, meaning that individual choices cannot be predetermined. Their responses to

this test have real-life problems. From a religious point of view, for example, people's choices could lead to either

destiny damnation or salvation. From a scientific perspective, high sugar intake could lead to a disease such as

cancer. Or there might be other possible factors that can cause the disease. In the end, all choices are rooted in

the belief in free will or in a predetermined choice.

B. Write a summary of the passage in your own words.

Vocabulary in Context

A. Complete the conversation below with vocabulary from the passage.

damnation   sins   analogy   determined   destiny

A: Who was at the door?

B: Oh, one of those people threatening me with eternal _____¹.

A: Eternal what?

B: You know, going to Hell for all my _____².

A: But if they are right, your _____³ can be changed.

B: Or maybe it has already been _____⁴. It's like a game of chess.

A: Nice _____⁵. I get the similarity.

B. Choose the sentences where the underlined words have the same meanings as they do in the passage.

1. a. Split bamboo can be used as ropes for tying a raft.

   b. Public opinion on the issue of free medical care was still split after the last poll.

2. a. Tourism has been both a salvation and a curse for this beautiful little island.

   b. Before his execution, the criminal prayed for his salvation.

3. a. Most respondents in the latest poll indicated they would vote for Mr. Johansson.

   b. Mr. Smith appeared in court on behalf of all the respondents in this case.

C. Complete the chart below by writing phrases with the word "cake" based on the definitions on the left. Then, write sentences using the phrases.

Definition	Phrase
1. something very easy to do	a piece of cake
2. to be sold quickly	
3. something that makes a situation even better	
4. a portion of the profits	

1. *The college entrance exam is not exactly **a piece of cake**.*

2. _____

3. _____

4. _____

Reading Connections

Read the following passage about the prisoner's dilemma. Then, do the exercises.

🎧 28

The Prisoner's Dilemma

Newcomb's Problem is sometimes associated with the prisoner's dilemma, another famous philosophical paradox. While Newcomb's Problem is a question of free will, the prisoner's dilemma asks how one should balance self-interest against cooperation for mutual gain. To understand the prisoner's dilemma, consider the following example.

Two criminals named Dave and Gary are arrested under suspicion of committing a bank robbery. The police do not have any evidence to charge either Dave or Gary with the robbery. Instead, they interrogate both suspects individually and offer each one a bargain, hoping one of the two will incriminate the other. If Dave and Gary both incriminate each other, both will be sentenced to two years in prison. If Dave betrays Gary but Gary remains silent, Dave will go free, and Gary will be sentenced to three years in prison, and vice-versa. However, if Dave and Gary both remain silent, they will each be sentenced to only one year in prison for possession of a handgun.

The paradox of the prisoner's dilemma is this: Both criminals can minimize their total jail time to a total of 2 years only if they both co-operate, but the incentives that they each face separately will always encourage them each to incriminate the other and end up being sentenced to 4 years, which is the maximum combined jail time.

The prisoner's dilemma has seen many manifestations in real life, such as the behavior of countries engaged in economic agreements. Whereas it may be more beneficial for all participating countries to cooperate, individual interests will always encourage one of the participants in the agreement to cheat in some way in order to extract a greater economic benefit.

Making Inferences
Check (✓) the statements that can be inferred from the above passage.

1. Neither the prisoner's dilemma nor Newcomb's Problem are paradoxical. ☐

2. In the prisoner's dilemma, Dave and Gary have no incentive to remain silent. ☐

3. Either Gary or Dave will be motivated by personal benefit to incriminate the other. ☐

4. The combined penalty for mutual incrimination is higher than that for keeping silent. ☐

5. Countries that engage in economic agreements are faced with the prisoner's dilemma. ☐

Reflections   According to the prisoner's dilemma, people will always try to maximize profits. If that is the case, is the saying "You can't trust anyone" true? Can we ever trust anyone?